TAROT FOR LIFE

TAROT FOR LIFE

by

Prospero

AEON

First published 2004
by Aeon Books
London W5
www.aeonbooks.co.uk

© Prospero 2004
The moral right of the author has been asserted

All rights reserved. No part of this book may be reproduced or utilized in any form or by any means, electronic or mechanical, without permission in writing from the publisher.

British Library Cataloguing in Publication Data

A C.I.P. is available for this book from the British Library

ISBN 1 904658 03 2

Printed and bound in Great Britain

For Sue,
Who brought her Sunshine
Into my Garden
And let it Grow.

ACKNOWLEDGEMENTS

Too many people have contributed to the making of this book for me to acknowledge them all individually. However, the following are particularly worthy of honourable mention.

Sue, the Muse Incarnate;

John and Patricia Hanshaw, my parents, for teaching me the value of original thinking;

Sprogger, Bel, Lumpkin, the various Hounds, Cats and Rodents, bringers of joy into my darkest hours;

Paul Hughes-Barlow, fellow Tarot author, whose writing process was six months ahead of mine and who shared generously his time, ideas and contacts;

Andrew Smith, Bill Hearn, Avis McKinney, Mark Dunn, Arthur Hopkins and Bob France, fellow travellers on the Royal Road of Tarot;

Nat Chait, Joe Carter, Seán Russell Friend, Stephanie Willis, Stu Lancaster, Ian Threadgill, Kieron Callow, Mark Coffey, Beryl Stockman, Wendy Katz, Chris Hoffen and John Precedo, fellow travellers on the rather bumpier Road of Life;

George Levy, master clarinettist and teacher, whose insight into music and the learning process gave me both inspiration for the work and a productive respite from it;

Roy and Sophie Gee and friends, Matt Oldfield, Sue and Sam and guests at the Rock, Barry and guests at the Ranelagh, for supplying the soundtrack to the writing process;

Oliver Rathbone, Jayanthi Perera, Kate Levy, Ryan Kennedy and all at Merton Abbey Mills, for help and encouragement in the difficult business of making a living from Tarot;

Alan and all at the Dragon, Kemp Town, for fuelling the fires of creation in a congenial environment.

ABOUT THE AUTHOR

Prospero is a full-time Tarot reader and teacher living and working in Brighton, England. He first became interested in Tarot after a series of bizarre experiences during a major illness that led him to question what he now refers to as his "default atheism". He has explored various psychic and occult disciplines, but Tarot remains, to him, the most complete and satisfying.

Outside working hours, Prospero is a keen amateur clarinettist and saxophonist. He shares his life with Mrs Prospero and their pet rats. When not at home or work, he can usually be found in one of Brighton's several excellent jazz clubs.

Contents

LESSON ZERO　　　　　　　　　　　　　　　　1
An Overview of the Course
Your First Spread
The Fool
Exercise 0: Journeying

LESSON ONE:　　　　　　　　　　　　　　　　8
The Structure Of The Tarot
The Fifteen-Card Romany Spread
The Magician
The Four Aces
Exercise I: Manifesting

LESSON TWO:　　　　　　　　　　　　　　　　16
Meditating With Tarot Cards
The Ba Gua Spread
The High Priestess
The Four Twos
Exercise II: Moving To Now

LESSON THREE: 22
A Short History
The Houses Spread
The Empress
The Four Threes
Exercise III: Wishes

LESSON FOUR: 28
A Map Of The Self
The Emperor
The Four Fours
Exercise IV: Facing Fear

LESSON FIVE: 33
The Hierophant
The Four Fives
Exercise V: Contacting a Guide

LESSON SIX: 39
The Lovers
The Four Sixes
Exercise VI: Finding The Teachers

LESSON SEVEN: 44
The Chariot
The Four Sevens
Exercise VII: Who's Pulling Your Strings

LESSON EIGHT: 50
Strength
The Four Eights
Exercise VIII: Finding Your Strengths

LESSON NINE: 55
Tarot As A Memory Aid
The Hermit
The Four Nines
Exercise IX: The Why Game

LESSON TEN: 62
Astrology and the Tarot
The Wheel of Fortune
The Four Tens
Exercise X: Talking To Aliens

LESSON ELEVEN: 68
Ethics
Justice
The Four Pages
Exercise XI: Disarming The Enemy

LESSON TWELVE: 76
The Hanged Man
The Four Knights
Exercise XII: Affirmations (With a Twist)

LESSON THIRTEEN: 83
Death
The Four Queens
Exercise XIII: Playing With Time

LESSON FOURTEEN: 89
Temperance
The Four Kings
Exercise XIV: Never Say Never

LESSON FIFTEEN: 96
Some challenges
The Devil
Exercise XV: Making It Happen

LESSON SIXTEEN: 101
The Tower
Exercise XVI: The Rant

LESSON SEVENTEEN: 106
The Star
Exercise XVII: Recognizing The Species

LESSON EIGHTEEN: 112
The Moon
Exercise XVIII: Acting Out

LESSON NINETEEN: 117
The Sun
Exercise XIX: Reasons To Be Cheerful

LESSON TWENTY: 121
Judgement
Exercise XX: Personal Aeonics

LESSON TWENTY ONE: 126
Reading Professionally
The World
Exercise XXI: Sharing Consciousness

Afterword: The Menu 133

Appendix I - Aleister Crowley and the Law of Thelema 134

Appendix II - Constructing the Inner Temple 140

Lesson Zero

Give me the courage to change what I can,
The serenity to accept what I cannot change,
And the wisdom to know the difference.
-Prayer attributed to Saint Augustine

It may seem odd to start a course on Tarot with a Christian prayer, but no words I have seen express the value of good Tarot reading better. In every life there are things that can be adjusted for better results and other things that must be accepted as they are. Used well, Tarot can illustrate both and help us to exercise more freedom of choice in our lives. Used badly, it too often gives the impression that there is no choice and that we are 'fated' to go along a certain path.

One of the biggest misconceptions about Tarot, and one of the main causes of bad reading practice, is the idea that reading the cards is a matter of learning a set of fixed meanings and then applying them rigidly to all people and all situations. It is as if Tarot were a computer code, a matter of cold logic. Tarot is a language of sorts, certainly, and any language must have a certain amount of structure and rigidity to have meaning.

However, in order to have continuing value, a language must be flexible enough for each of its speakers to 'customise' it to their own needs.

So, if the cards are a language, who, or what, is speaking? Gareth Knight, a writer I hold in high esteem, talks about a 'Spirit of the Tarot', which is a valuable idea. Whether we see this Spirit as an outer entity, or as an aspect of our own subconscious, matters little in practice. What matters is that, by relating to the Tarot as if it were a wise old friend offering advice, we can hold the appropriate attitude, respectful but not subservient, able and willing to read between the lines of what is said and to filter it through our own common sense.

So, in that spirit, it gives me great pleasure to introduce you to my friend the Tarot. May its acquaintance bring as much joy and wisdom into your life as it has into mine.

An Overview of the Course

This course developed from the face-to-face courses I have taught and, while the sequence of events may seem a little illogical, it has been found to work well in practice. If you work with the lessons in the order given, resisting the urge to peek at later lessons, your experience will be as similar as I can get in a book to that which turns out students I am proud of on the face-to-face courses.

Each lesson contains the following:

Some practical information, either about the structure of the Tarot or how to use it in readings or in other ways;
A spread you can use, with some idea of where it can be most useful;
Card descriptions ~ one Major Arcana card in each lesson and four Minor Arcana in each of lessons I to XIV;
An exercise based on the Major Arcana card for the lesson.

I would suggest that you first read through the entire lesson. In some cases, for example 'A Map of the Self' in Lesson IV, the first section is conceptual and need only be read and understood once. In other cases, you may find it useful (though it is not essential) to memorise this section.

The spreads should be tried at least once. It is not necessary to memorise them. You will find that some work well for you while others seem less useful. In practice, most readers have one or two spreads that they use most of the time and perhaps a couple of others for particular situations. If you do not feel confident enough to read for others at this early stage, or if you lack sufficient volunteers, then read for imaginary clients in your practice sessions.

The card descriptions should be seen as an introduction. By the time you read the later ones you should be forming your own notions of what the individual cards are about. If my ideas help to flesh out your own, that is fine. If they seem to contradict your own understanding, ignore them.

The final exercise is meant to show you the self-development aspect of the Tarot. This wonderful tool was surely designed to give much more than divination alone. I hope you gain some useful insights from these exercises.

While it is perfectly possible to complete the course alone, you may find it a more enjoyable and rewarding experience to do so in a group. I would suggest no more than six people. It is important to have a coordinator, perhaps alternating this role to avoid one person being overworked or appearing overly egotistical. In my face-to-face courses I have seen some very worthwhile friendships develop among my students.

Grounding and Shielding

This exercise is recommended for use before a reading or series of readings. Its purpose is to create a state in which you are open to receive information psychically but closed to the energy-draining effect that can take place when you open up to a person in need. Remember, we are all capable of being 'psychic vampires', especially when upset or anxious, and it is not usually deliberate. If you want to give energy to someone, do it deliberately. Energy given freely is far more useful to them and less of a drain on you.

Remember also that the link goes two ways. You may want or need to do a reading when you feel emotionally or physically drained or even in crisis. Taking energy from a client, or passing on negative energy to them, is more than just discourteous. It could completely undermine the purpose of the reading.

The exercise can also be used as a daily or twice-daily exercise for grounding, calmness, and protection. Since it is self-balancing, you cannot 'overdose' on it.

The system of colours used here works on the chakras, or energy centres, located at various points along the centre of the spine. Various colour schemes and formats exist for working on the chakras. This is not 'the one true way'; it is simply the method I find most helpful for the purposes given above.

Sit or stand in a comfortable position with arms and legs uncrossed. Start to breathe long, regular deep breaths from the diaphragm. If you have a breathing rhythm you particularly like, learned from Yoga or some other discipline, by all means use it.

Visualise roots going down from the base of your spine and the arch of each foot straight into the floor. Let them go straight down, thick and strong, forty feet or more into the ground. This is the 'grounding' part. If you ever feel unpleasantly 'spaced out', it is legitimate to use this part on its own.

Now imagine energy coming up through your roots into your body. As it enters your body, it takes on a bright red colour until it reaches the waist.

At the waist the energy turns to orange for two or three inches, then turns yellow at a point above the navel. From the base of the ribcage to the base of the throat, including the arms and hands, the energy is green.

The last three chakras are especially important from a reading point of view. The throat should be light blue. Then, for the first time, we allow a break in the colour scheme and place a dark blue band around the forehead. The last colour, covering the crown of the head, is a rich violet.

Now imagine the energy turning white, again from the feet up, this time covering the whole of the body. Imagine your body shining with white light.

Finally, the 'shielding'. Imagine an oval-shaped shell of white light around your body, about a foot out in all directions. This is a strengthening of a shield, which is there anyway but benefits from your visualisation. If you ever feel seriously threatened by an 'atmosphere' or feel psychically 'threatened', you can turn this auric shell reflective silver for extra protection. Remember to turn it back to white when the threat is gone, though. The silver is an absolute block on all energy exchange and is not healthy for long-term use.

Your First Spread

The spread shown is about the simplest, short of a 'one carder', but is surprisingly versatile and useful. To use it, simply shuffle the cards and lay out three from the top of the deck in the order shown. It can be used to look at a particularly important event in the future, a particular period of time or a particular question. It can be used as a basis for free-form extensions if a question turns out to be more complex than anticipated.

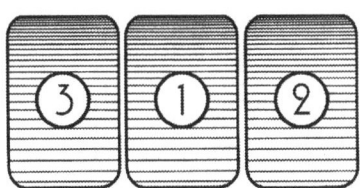

Once you have laid out the cards, take a moment to absorb impressions from them. Feel what the images are trying to tell you. Is their message one of hope or caution? If there are court cards, representing people, do they look friendly, unfriendly or neutral?

Feel free to link cards to any known information about the issue. For example, if you are reading for the next day's events and you know you are likely to have an important discussion with your boss, it is not 'cheating' to recognise that as the significance of the Emperor.

When you have extracted all you can from the cards directly, then you can look at 'book meanings' if you wish. If you find the two in conflict, though, follow your own instincts. The only one who has the last word on your relationship to the cards is you.

The Fool

Paradoxically, The Fool stands for wisdom, but it is wisdom of a special kind. This is the wisdom of the Holy Fool, who knows how to forget himself and simply be. It is the wisdom that cuts in when we do not have time to think, or when we deliberately stop thinking in meditation.

Eastern spiritual teachers often characterise the conscious mind as a monkey. In this card it is often shown as a small, excited dog. These are useful images for the chattering, easily distracted creature that has its home between our ears. How often are we really present in our bodies, living our lives, here and now? For most of us, I suspect, this state only occurs in moments of great excitement, rapture, or danger. It is sometimes known as Gnosis and one of the goals of mysticism is to reach it on a continuous basis. It is possible, though far from easy, to live our entire lives this way.

The Fool's number is 0, the number that initiates the sequence of numbers. He has nothing and knows that he is nothing. He sees through the illusions of daily life and can play in this world because he knows it is not real.

In divination, the Fool stands for new ventures and adventures, for stepping out into the unknown. In terms of our day-to-day needs this can be a smart move or a stupid one. Whatever else we gain or lose from doing this, we gain experience. We also gain that beautiful moment at the beginning when we can say, in all sincerity, 'I know nothing'.

Exercise 0: Journeying

I love travelling. Even the shortest journey out of my familiar environment brings the excitement of new knowledge and a feeling of 'making it mine'. Setting out on a motorcycle with a week free and a passport in my pocket is one of the best feelings I know.

But what about the routine journeys? Can the daily hike to the office or the supermarket offer us anything worthwhile? Yes, I believe they can.

Next time you undertake such a journey, try to imagine that you are a tourist. The door of your house or flat is the door of your hotel. Try to get the feel of the place as you would a new location. Notice the architecture, the light, the mood and attire of the people in the street. Compare what you are seeing to other places you have visited. Does your part of town feel like London, Paris, New York?

The same approach can be applied to a single building, a single room, a person, or even an object. Looking at an old musical instrument, say, as if you have just bought it can add to the pleasure of playing it. Try it with anything, man-made or natural, simple or complex.

Lesson One

The Structure of the Tarot

The Tarot deck is divided into two sections, the twenty-two Major Arcana (or Trumps) and the Minor Arcana, which are further divided into four suits, Wands (or Rods), Cups, Swords and Pentacles (or coins). (A pentacle, by the way, is a plate used in ritual magick.) Each suit has four court cards (King, Queen, Knight and Page) and ten 'pip' cards.

The Major Arcana

These are the 'movers and shakers' of the Tarot deck. Their emphasis is on inner consciousness rather than external life events but when they turn up in force in a spread it indicates a pattern of destiny that is very difficult or impossible to break, but which will provide many lessons and revelations if seen in the right way.

Collectively, the Major Arcana can be used as a map of human consciousness. Each card has an attribution linking it to a planet, sign or element. Everyone has a full set of planets and signs in their chart, as well as all of the character components represented by them. To own and use all of these elements as one organic whole is the task referred to by the psychologist as integration and by the occultist as The Great Work.

The Four Suits

These are strongly linked to the four Elements, sometimes referred to as the Aristotelian Elements, which represent the four 'levels' in everything that exists; a recurrent theme throughout Western esoteric thought.

Fire represents the fundamental energy of things, the vitality and movement of life. It is represented in the Tarot by Judgment and the suit of Wands.

Water represents the emotional and the creative/intuitive level. It is represented in the Tarot by the Hanged Man and the suit of Cups.

Air represents the mental level, intellect, reasoning and logic. It is represented in the Tarot by the Fool and the suit of Swords.

Earth represents the physical level, the body, money, material possessions and the outer, physical world. It is represented by the World (arguably) and the suit of Pentacles.

For this book, for example, Fire represents the enthusiasm necessary for me to write these words and for you to read them. Water represents the emotions involved for both of us and the creative process of forming my ideas into words. Air represents the intellectual ideas I am trying to pass on. Earth represents the physical mechanism by which the words are transmitted, the hardware and software involved.

For reading purposes, the suits have broad areas of relevance based on this structure:

The Wands refer to work and career, that which (at least in theory) ought to be done with energy and enthusiasm;

The Cups refer to the emotional life, especially to romance. They are possibly the most overworked cards in the deck;

The Swords refer to the intellect but are also the 'bad news' suit, perhaps because, although intellect alone is seldom enough to get us through, it can create the dangerous illusion that we have 'covered all the angles';

The Pentacles refer to matters of money and wealth and to the physical body.

This is only a broad guide, with many diversions in practice. The Swords in particular can refer to almost any area of life.

The Court Cards

These cards often represent people. The Kings and Queens represent mature men and women respectively, the Knights young men and the Pages young women or children. In some decks the Knight becomes a Prince and the Page a Princess, in which case I would divide children by gender.

The court cards can also represent stages in an experience. For example, the Page of Wands might turn up to represent a new job or the King to represent the peak of someone's career.

The Pip Cards

Here we come to another aspect of the Tarot's multiple sets of associations. The pip cards can most easily be understood by reference to the Spheres of the Tree of Life, but we will learn more about this later. For now, if you do not know about the Tree, do not worry about the unfamiliar names. Simply imagine each set of cards emerging from the last and you will get the general sense of what I am trying to convey.

The Aces are linked to Kether, and represent the energy of their suit in its purest possible form. As Kether is the first Sphere to emerge from the Void, so the Aces represent new beginnings. To me, the Aces also indicate that, given reasonable effort, what is begun is certain of success. This distinguishes them from the 'beginning' aspect of the Pages, where there is a stronger element of uncertainty.

The Twos are linked to Chokmah and represent force in potential, as yet devoid of a form to act upon. They might be described as the pause before action.

The Threes are linked to Binah and represent a first 'completion point'. Here we see fulfilment of at least part of the promise of the Ace and Two, though not necessarily the happiest part.

The Fours are linked to Chesed and represent a stable state, a resting point if you will.

The Fives are linked to Geburah, the Sphere linked to Mars, in which things are cut down to the essentials. They all represent trouble of one kind or another.

The Sixes are linked to Tipareth, the Sphere at the heart of the Tree, and have an expansive, optimistic quality.

The Sevens are linked to Netzach and are sharply divided. Wands and Cups are cautiously optimistic, while Swords and Pentacles present a gloomy picture.

The Eights, linked to Hod, are again divided. The Wands, Cups and Pentacles present neutral or positive activity, while the Eight of Swords represents restriction and delay at best.

The Nines, linked to Yesod, show very negative in Wands and Swords but powerfully positive in Cups and Pentacles.

The Tens, the conclusion in Malkuth, repeat this pattern even more emphatically.

The Fifteen-Card Romany Spread

This is my favourite spread for general readings. I find it gives plenty of scope for the cards to express the essence of a complex situation but keeps things contained enough to avoid fuzzy generalities.

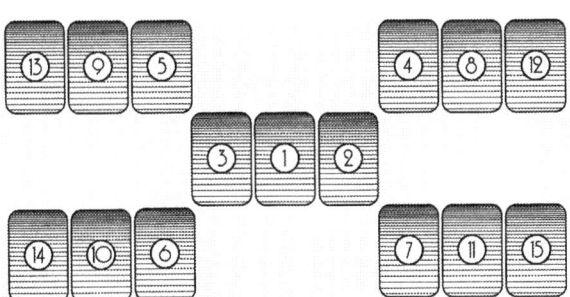

Cards 7, 11 and 15 represent what the querent is bringing to the situation. They may show innate character traits, factors from childhood or the tone of the querent's life so far.

Cards 6, 10 and 14 show the recent past, the backdrop to the present.

Cards 1, 2 and 3 show the present and near future events, normally within three months.

Cards 4, 8 and 12 show the natural future, i.e. events as they are most likely to transpire.

Cards 5, 9 and 13 are called the 'alternative future'. They may show a complete alternative path (useful if the Natural Future looks grim) or extra events which can be brought in, but these may be positive or negative. They should also show a difference in the querent's own action, which is required to bring about 'alternative' events.

The Magician

The Magician might be regarded as twin brother to the Fool, the other half of a dynamic equation that requires both to be present before either makes sense. The Fool's glory is that he knows nothing and therefore has perfect faith. The Magician's is that he knows all he needs to know. In many decks he stands with one hand raised, pointing to Heaven, the other pointing down to Earth. He acts as mediator between the two, knowing both. In some older decks such as the Marseilles he appears as a juggler, a natural counterpoint to the clown. In ancient times many different skills were regarded as sacred mysteries. Smiths, carpenters and craftsmen of all kinds formed Guilds or Companies to preserve their secrets. Today, the Freemasons are a surviving relic of that time. To be a 'magician' then was a matter of doing something so well that it became a sacred art.

His astrological attribution is Mercury, the planet of knowledge and communication.

The Aces

As I said earlier in this lesson, the Aces represent the purest and therefore the strongest energy of their suit. We might see in this the strength of 'purity of intent', where purity refers not to morality but to single-minded focus on a goal.

The Ace of Wands

Linking the ideas covered earlier, we can see that the Ace of Wands brings together the idea of pure or new action with that of career, in which career is more than just a means of earning money.

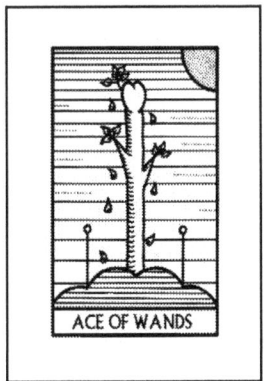

Thus, in a reading, the Ace of Wands represents a change at the work level and a decisive move towards doing something for a living that more accurately reflects the individual's unique character.

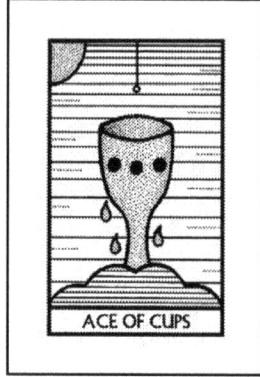

The Ace of Cups

The Ace of Cups brings its strength to the area of emotion and creativity. In a reading it stands for a new creative impetus. This will often take the form of falling in love and starting a new relationship. Even where there is an established relationship, it can often act as a channel for a new influx of creativity.

The Ace of Swords

This card speaks of new ideas and efforts to learn. It is the classic card for a course of study, whether for student or teacher.

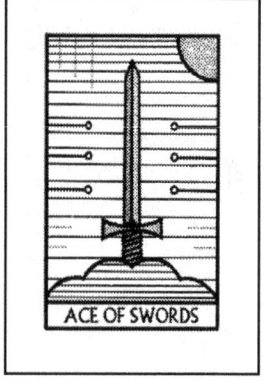

The Ace of Swords stands for single-mindedness and strength of purpose. This holds true for any of the aces to some extent, but this one illustrates most clearly the saying 'Nothing is more dangerous than an idea when it is the only one you have.' When everything we are and everything in us is devoted to a single goal, we can achieve anything.

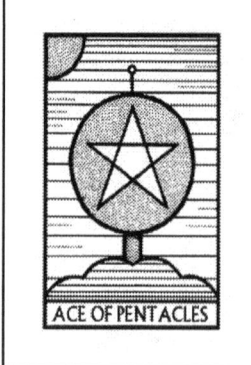

The Ace of Pentacles

The Ace of Pentacles has to cover a wide range of events, dealing with a combination of new beginnings in the realms of health, money and the physical. An improvement in financial status, a change of home and a birth are all potential meanings, depending on other cards around it. In questions of health it would be a strong positive indication.

Exercise I: Manifesting

Magick can be as complicated as you like, but the essence of it is extremely simple. Peter Carroll summed it up nicely with his phrase 'sleight of mind'. Impress an idea deep enough into your subconscious and it will start to manifest in outer reality.

The best way to prove this to yourself is by practical experiment. Don't try for earth-shattering results at first. A good example of the level to aim at would be finding your favourite sandwich available when you go to lunch. Another would be finding an ideal parking place.

Now take a few minutes to visualise the result you have chosen. Bring in as many senses as possible. This is one of the reasons I like food-based examples; food has something to offer all of the physical senses. Enjoy this part of the process as much as possible. When it feels as complete and as real as you can make it, gradually return to here and now, focussing on tactile sensations and sounds before opening your eyes.

The last part of the process is simply to put yourself where the experience concerned can happen. If your visualisation was a sandwich, it is unlikely to fulfill itself unless you go somewhere where sandwiches are available.

If the first attempt does not produce instant results, simply keep trying until the goal is achieved. The next goal will come more quickly. Like most worthwhile activities, manifesting takes practice.

Lesson Two

Meditating With Tarot Cards

There are several different methods of meditating with Tarot cards. Some of the more 'active' forms, depending heavily on imagination and visualisation, will be dealt with later on. For now, a simpler approach will be more productive.

Start by choosing a card. I would suggest that you limit your selection to the Major Arcana for now. You may choose the card either intuitively - by shuffling - or by going in a numerical sequence.

Read my commentary on the card you have selected, along with any other material you have on it. Then take the card out and look at it for ten minutes or so. Ask yourself how it connects with experiences or people in your life and aspects of your own personality. Look at the imagery. See how it might connect to what you have read about the card and what other ideas it might suggest. Mentally invite the card to reveal itself to you through the events of the day.

Do this once or twice a day and note the events of the day. I guarantee they will show you the essence of the card in action. It is worth keeping a journal during this type of work to note down any insights.

Incidentally, this is why I suggest sticking to the Major Arcana. None of these cards are inherently negative, even though some of the energies they represent can be more easily mismanaged than others.

A useful variation on this technique is to use the cards for dream incubation. For this type of work, a journal is essential rather than merely useful. The procedure is essentially the same as above, except that you should meditate immediately before going to bed and try to hold a mental image of the card as you drift off to sleep.

The Ba Gua Spread

This spread comes into its own when doing short readings one after the other, for example at a party. It is also a useful example of how you can make spreads up for yourself. I came up with it from looking at the Ba Gua grid in Denise Linn's excellent book *Sacred Space*.

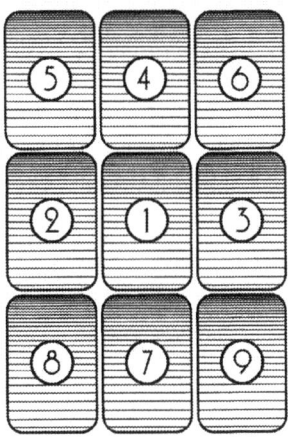

Card 1 is about health. Be aware that very negative cards here may be a reference to past problems or to emotional stress rather than an imminent physical health crisis.

Card 2 is about family and upbringing.

Card 3 is about children and projects.

Card 4 is about self-expression, image and, if relevant, fame.

Card 5 is about wealth and money.
Card 6 is about relationships.
Card 7 is about career.
Card 8 is about inner growth.
Card 9 is about helpful people.

There are some useful cross-references here. For instance, I often view cards 5 and 7 together, sometimes bringing in card 3 or 4, depending on the querent's career aspirations.

The High Priestess

This is the first female card in the sequence of the Major Arcana and is one of a 'natural pair' with the Hierophant. (The latter is also referred to as The High Priest, which is what 'hierophant' means anyway, and in French decks they are usually Le Pape and La Papesse.) The High Priestess refers to secrets and mysteries. In many decks she is shown sitting in front of a curtain between two pillars, guarding secret knowledge from the profane. One pillar is usually black, the other white, indicating the equilibrium of Yin and Yang or male and female. Her femininity can be taken as indicating her 'inner' quality, the part within that must be looked for inside each of us.

Another aspect of this card is that she is usually dressed in blue, a point in common with the Virgin Mary in a lot of religious artwork. This seems unlikely to be accidental. It is interesting to note that Roman Catholics, who worship a triune male god under an exclusively male priesthood, sometimes refer to 'Mother Church'.

The Twos

In the last lesson I described the Twos as the pause before action. They represent force in abeyance. There is no high drama here, though the stillness of the Twos can be either calming or irritating, as we shall see.

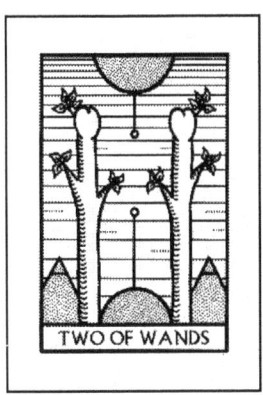

The Two of Wands

Many versions of this card show a man gazing pensively into the distance, holding a globe of the world or a crystal ball. When I see this card I think of the time at the beginning of a project. There may be little happening on the surface but hopes and fears are being weighed up and plans made. The globe sometimes gives this card a connotation of travel. When this is so, it is never a routine business trip or package holiday. This is a card of high adventure waiting to happen.

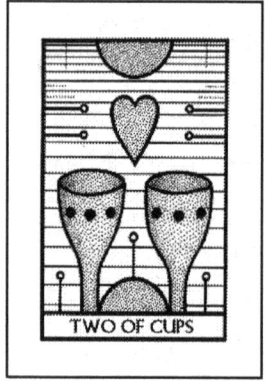

The Two of Cups
This card relates to love, but a specific kind of love. The partner is seen as different from the self and enjoyed as such. There is mutual respect as well as affection. When this state is reached, there is no power struggle. Easy to say, perhaps, and harder to find and live by, but it can be done. When it is, the relationship becomes a powerful source of creative energy for both parties.

The Two of Swords
Indecision. The querent sees both sides of the question and hangs back from action. Often this is a matter of self-doubt; the querent knows intuitively which way to go but lacks the confidence to take the first step.

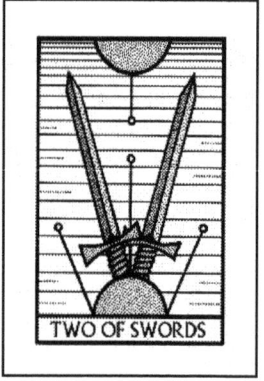

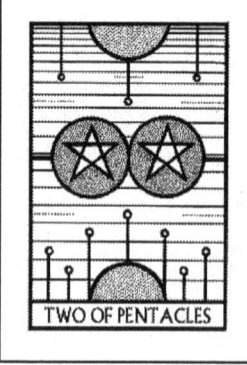

The Two of Pentacles
Uncertainties over money or the 'neither-nor' financial state in which most of us find ourselves some of the time, where there is no major financial hardship, but still the funds are insufficient to fulfill the heart's desire.

Exercise II: Moving To Now
This exercise is based on recent personal experience. I moved into my present home a year ago. It is the first I have owned after a succession of rented flats and the first place I have lived in since early childhood that feels like home. Making it into the home I want it to be is taking time, but is teaching me much about myself.

The latest lesson was about paper. I decided to go through every piece of paper in the flat and throw as much away as possible. As a typical Cancerian (translation: human packrat) the process is not yet complete and I have not got rid of as much as I expected, yet it has been immensely therapeutic. The flat seems somehow more light and airy and I feel as if I have taken off a heavy overcoat.

Part of this is the effect of getting rid of physical objects that linked me to the past. Less of me is held back there and more is available in the present. Whether this is a matter of subtle energies or psychology (or, as I think, both) is a fascinating but irrelevant question.

So the exercise is this. Find the redundant objects that you hoard and dispose of them in an appropriate fashion. Notice whatever emotions these objects bring up. Notice also the space you free up in your home and your mind and any changes in your physical energy level.

Lesson Three

A Short History

This bit is not really required information for the practice of reading the cards. I find it interesting and I hope you will too. If not, feel free to skip it and move on to The Empress.

Strange as it may seem, the known history of the Tarot only goes back as far as the late fourteenth century. Even stranger, the first known reference to the cards describes them purely as a gaming deck, with no mention of their occult or fortune-telling uses at all. It is at least possible that this wonderful tool started its life as nothing more exalted than a new toy for gamblers. Certainly their structural similarity to playing cards suggests this, though there is equally strong evidence for other theories, as we shall see.

Another now-popular tool for spiritual development, which emerged into the public domain at around the same time, was Kabalah, with its fascinating glyph, the Tree of Life. This system of thought emerged from the Jewish community in Southern Europe and had a strong appeal for many Christian scholars. Its alleged use by Biblical figures made it more acceptable to the Church than some other systems and its great versatility as a system of coding and classification gave it great appeal to many Renaissance scholars.

There are many parallels between Tarot and Kabalah. For example:

The Tree of Life has ten Sephiroth, or Spheres	The Tarot has ten numbered cards in each suit
These are connected by twenty-two paths corresponding to the letters of the Hebrew alphabet	There are twenty-two cards in the Major Arcana
There are four Worlds in Kabalah	There are four suits in the Minor Arcana and four court cards in each

These similarities caught the imagination of various Masonic and Rosicrucian thinkers, including Eliphas Levi, a French Catholic priest who wrote several books on magic in the nineteenth century. His work in turn helped to inspire S. L. 'Macgregor' Mathers, who along with Dr W. Wynn Westcott, founded the Hermetic Order of the Golden Dawn in 1887. The Order came to include such notables as A. E. Waite and Pamela Colman Smith (the author and artist executant of the Rider Waite deck), Dion Fortune and W. B. Yeats. It gave Aleister Crowley his first grounding in occultism and laid the foundation not only for large chunks of his system but also for much of what is now widely known as the Western Mystery Tradition.

The Golden Dawn was a closed order but, ironically, the rifts that finally broke it apart meant that its knowledge became public. Much of the more systematic information in this course and other books on Tarot is based on Golden Dawn sources.

The Houses Spread

This spread can be used for character readings, much like a natal chart in astrology, or as a general check-up for somebody who has no major issues at the time. As the name suggests, each card represents one of the astrological houses, though the areas of relevance are considerably curtailed from the more complex framework used in astrology.

These are:
1. Self-expression and outer image.
2. Wealth and material possessions.
3. Communication.
4. The home.
5. Play, creativity and children.
6. Health and day-to-day routine.
7. Partnerships.
8. Sexuality.
9. Philosophy, spirituality and higher education.
10. Career in the long-term sense.
11. Social life.
12. The unconscious and matters of secrecy.

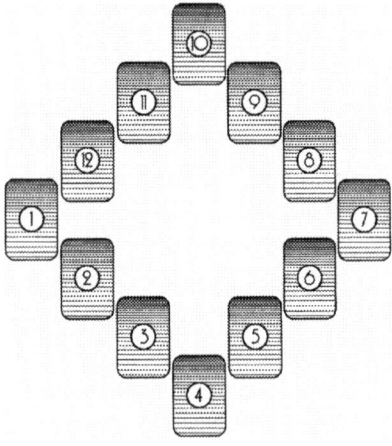

The Empress

As with the High Priestess, the Empress is one of a natural pair, obviously with the Emperor. This pair deals with temporal aspects of life, compared to the more spiritual aspects of the High Priestess and Hierophant.

Specifically, the Empress stands for fertility and beauty. She is usually shown as an attractive woman, often pregnant, in a natural setting among symbols of abundance such as ripe corn.

Of course most people today are not often directly concerned with issues of fertility in the literal sense. The card's astrological attribution to Venus gives us a broader perspective, taking in creativity, inspiration and achievement through cooperation rather than aggression. The saying 'Work smart, not hard' seems apt for the Empress's value in modern life, especially where 'smart' refers to intuitive rather than logical thinking.

The Threes
The Threes are associated with Binah, the end of the first part of the journey down the Tree of Life. As such they have a definite feel of completion about them, though this is not always a positive thing.

The Three of Wands

This card often shows a man standing in a high place watching ships in the distance. To me this is a card of partial reward, a stage successfully completed. Since it is a Wands card, this could be a promotion or the completion of a project.

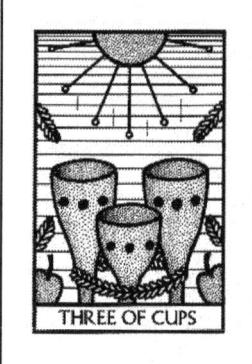

The Three of Cups

A straightforward card of celebration and positivity. A chance to relax, if only briefly. Often this card simply denotes a successful outcome.

The Three of Swords

The three swords are often shown running through a heart. This is a card of heartbreak, often with an element of betrayal.

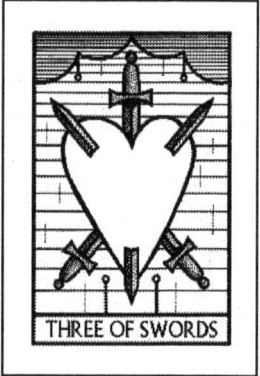

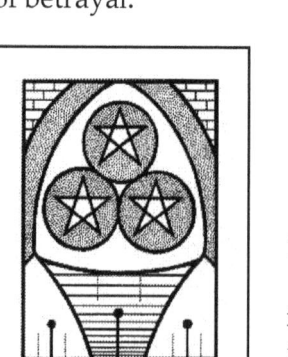

The Three of Pentacles

This card refers to money earned in a way that offers the worker satisfaction and pleasure. This is partly a matter of perception. Are you cutting stone or building a cathedral?

Exercise III: Wishes

This exercise is very simple in format but can be very complex in practice. Imagine that a genii or pixie or fairy godmother or whatever is standing before you offering you three wishes. Within the realms of the physically possible, you can ask for anything you want. So, for example, to ask to play the guitar like Segovia is fine but to ask to be able to fly without an aeroplane is not.

When you are reasonably happy with your list, simply ask yourself what you can do to bring those wishes closer to reality.

Lesson Four

A Map Of The Self

If the Tarot deck as a whole is a map of human life, then the Major Arcana are a map of the individual human psyche. The psychoanalyst C. G. Jung coined the term 'archetypes' to refer to different aspects of a personality which appear at different times. Jung formed his theories partly from a serious study of divinatory tools, including Tarot and Astrology, and to this day many Jungian analysts view the Major Arcana as the basic set of archetypes which each individual expresses or suppresses in his or her own unique pattern.

Although Jung put it into modern language and made it acceptable to some of us sceptical modern types, this idea is very old and underlies a good deal of practical occultism. Perhaps the clearest example of this is the work of G. I. Gurdjieff, who talked about different 'I's' and the necessity of uniting them into a single individual. Crowley's conception of the Great Work, while less explicitly stated, seems to drive at the same basic idea.

So how can we use this knowledge to help ourselves? Firstly, by simply looking at the map and identifying the aspects of ourselves that each card represents. We may find in the process that certain qualities are underused or even ignored altogether. Others may be taking too great a part in our actions. Even if you are fortunate enough to have a perfect balance among the different parts of yourself, labelling them in this way may make them more accessible when needed.

Another way of using this idea is to look at the people in your life, especially the ones who are giving you trouble of any kind or suffering themselves, and see which card best represents them. This will also represent an aspect of yourself which is not fully expressed. By finding a healthy and appropriate way to express it, you will also heal your connection to that person, enabling them to either relate to you more positively or pass out of your life.

The Mayan Spread

This is a spread I developed for use in telephone readings. Perhaps it would be more accurate to say that the spread developed itself over time. It has two advantages for that type of work. One is that it allows a large number of cards in a comparatively small space. The other is that it can be worked on a bit at a time, allowing you to start speaking almost immediately.

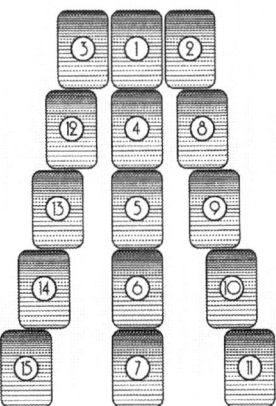

Lay out the first three cards at the beginning of the reading. The three sets of four cards tailing off from them are optional. You could lay them out in any order according to what the situation demands. This is what makes this spread so perfect for telephone work. A caller may have one simple question or want a detailed analysis of several interrelated life situations. This spread suits either situation.

Incidentally, the name has no mystical significance whatsoever. The shape just reminded me of a flat-topped Mayan pyramid.

The Emperor

The Emperor is, fairly obviously, the natural partner to the Empress. The card name suggests leadership and it does indeed signify the natural leader's qualities of logic, determination, assertiveness and forward thinking. Thus, the two cards can work together within us in a balanced way, but an excess of one of them at the expense of the other is likely to cost us dearly. A 'pure Empress' person would have wonderful dreams but would fall at the first hurdle in the real world. A 'pure Emperor' would be a bullying dictator with no imagination or spontaneity.

The Emperor's astrological attribution is Aries, the first and in a sense the simplest sign of the Zodiac. Aries is Cardinal Fire, pure energy in direct, uncomplicated motion. It knows where it is going and nothing can stand in its way.

In a spread the Emperor usually turns up when the querent is either taking on additional power and responsibility or confronting authority. At work this could be a promotion or a switch to self-employment. At home it is often a decision to stand up to a dominating partner or family. Either way there is a choice for more freedom but also a risk of arrogance and unnecessary strife.

The Fours

On the Tree, these cards fall under the expansive Jupiterian influence of Chesed. A gentle set, then, but not exclusively positive, as we shall see.

The Four of Wands

Somewhat out of kilter with the rest of the suit, I see this as a card of marriage. In these easygoing times we can broaden this out to cover any

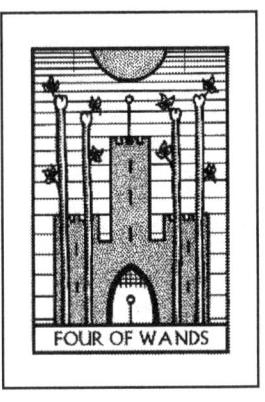

committed relationship. Of course, this need not be a personal relationship; sometimes a business contract is indicated. The key here is long-term stability.

The Four of Cups

A gift as yet unseen. This may be a gift or favour from another but is often the emergence of an unsuspected talent.

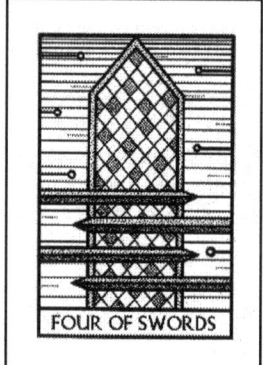

The Four of Swords
I see this card as peace and acceptance, though often in a 'no win' situation where compromise is accepted as a necessary evil.

The Four of Pentacles

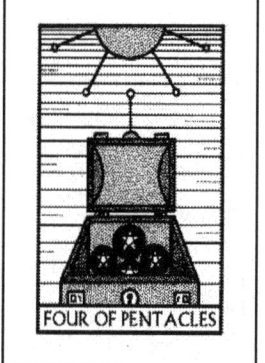

The illustration here is often a classic miser, someone who has plenty but is too afraid of loss to enjoy it. I see it as illusory problems over money, or perhaps real problems exaggerated by a fearful refusal to look too closely at the situation.

Exercise IV: Facing Fear

This is one to take in stages, and perhaps one to defer for later if you feel close to the edge emotionally or are suffering from mental illness.

Fear holds us back from more good things than any other single factor. When we conquer fear we eliminate some of the biggest barriers and energy drains in our lives.

Write down a list of your fears. They need not be anything debilitating; even something you never come up against in daily life will do. When you feel the list is as complete as you can make it, give each item a number according to its emotional charge.

Now simply work through the list, starting with the least emotionally charged item. If it is practical for you to experience the situation concerned directly in physical time, that is preferable. If that is not possible, or if it would require you to put yourself in unacceptable danger, visualise the experience as vividly as you can. Do this until the fear is either gone or reduced as far as it can be.

Lesson Five

Significators

Significators are a very strong feature of some people's reading style. I personally find little use for them but it is as well to know what they are and how to select them.

The usual procedure is to find out the querent's Sun sign. The element of that sign and the querent's age and gender define the court card to be used. Opinion varies as to what age defines the difference between a King or Queen and a Knight or Page. I would say this is an area in which to go by feeling. If the querent seems mature and well established in life, choose the King or Queen. If there is evidence of immaturity or a very youthful demeanour, choose the Knight or Page.

Thus, as a 38-year-old Cancerian male, I would be represented by either the King or the Knight of Cups.

Another kind of 'significator', which I do use occasionally, is a card chosen from one spread used as a focal point in another to clarify issues left unclear by the first. This could be any card in the deck, whichever best represents the area that you wish to clarify.

The Celtic Cross Spread

This is perhaps the best known of all Tarot spreads, largely because it was the favourite of A. E. Waite, a member of the Golden Dawn with little talent for Magick but much for publicity. Like his Tarot deck and his book on the subject, it does an adequate job for those with low aspirations. I find it extremely limiting. However, it is a good example of a spread using significators.

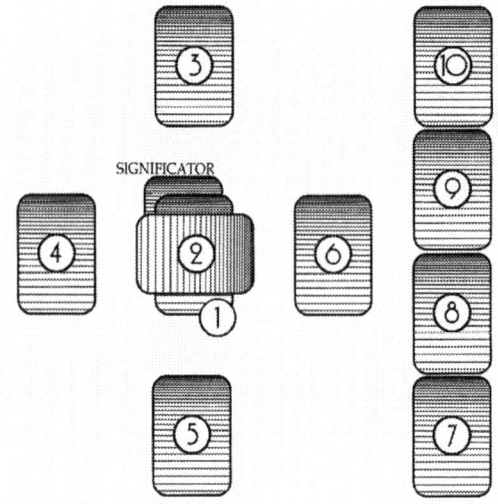

Choose your significator as mentioned earlier in this chapter. The other cards are read as follows:

1. The issue the querent is thinking about.
2. What crosses him.
3. The past.
4. The present.
5. Short term future.
6. Longer term future.
7. How the querent sees himself.
8. Friends or enemies.
9. Hopes and fears.
10. Outcome.

The Hierophant

The Hierophant is the last member in our pair of cosy couples, the counterpart to the High Priestess. As she goes inward, exploring the secret territory of our hearts and minds, the Hierophant brings this new knowledge out into the light.

This card often appears blatantly Christian and is sometimes even named The Pope. Perhaps in some ways he would be better titled The Parish Priest. His role is that of an advisor, a wise counsel with little temporal power but much authority through respect. Modern 'hierophants' would include counsellors, psychoanalysts and therapists of all kinds. Readers and psychics also fall into this role.

The Hierophant's astrological attribution is Taurus, reminding us that, no matter how lofty our ideals, we must bring them to fruition here on Earth before they can mean anything.

The Fives

The fives bring us to Geburah, the Sephirah linked to Mars. As you might expect, then, they have a quality that is trying at best and murderous at worst. The only thing we can do to get us past these points in life is to remember that 'this too will pass' and plough on.

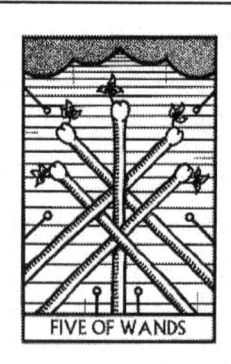

The Five of Wands

The most obvious kind of trouble; fights, arguments and squabbles, especially with people who are normally friendly contacts. This is not the most serious card of aggression. Unless others back it up, these issues can usually be sorted out.

The Five of Cups

An emotional focus on the negative, while the positive is unseen or underrated. A new take on the situation would alleviate or entirely remove the problems.

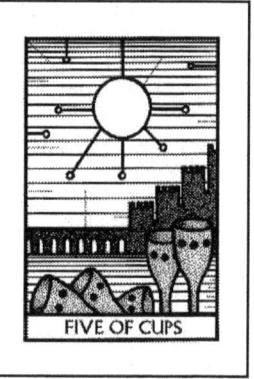

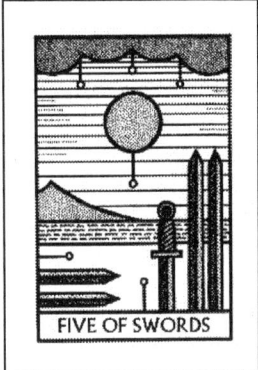

The Five of Swords
My take on this card is, I admit, unusual but it works for me. I see it as an advantage gained from others' problems. There is usually some guilt, even if it is not warranted.

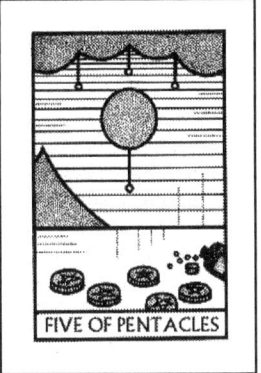

The Five of Pentacles
Problems with money or health. Unlike those of the Four, these are real problems and need attention.

Exercise V: Contacting A Guide
There is a school of thought, by no means confined to materialist psychologists, which says that the Spirit Guides encountered in the Spiritualist tradition are nothing more than fragments of the unconscious taking form in order to be heard by the conscious mind. From my own perspective this is a half-truth. At the ultimate level all the events which happen to us and the characters in them are our own creations. At a less exalted level my own experience with Guides suggests that, by and large, they are what they claim to be. Perhaps the distinction is irrelevant in practice. What matters is the quality of the advice and/or information they give us.

Making contact with a Guide is easier than you might imagine. It can take a while, though, so start by creating a physical space in which you can sit comfortably with no distractions for at least an hour. It is also important to sit with arms and legs uncrossed.

When you are reasonably relaxed physically, do the Grounding and Shielding exercise from Lesson 0, this time without opening your physical eyes at the end. Instead, open your inward eyes in an environment of your choosing, real or imaginary. My own favourite is a walled garden.

When you have the environment as clear as you can make it at this time, find a place for your Guide to appear. He or she may come through a gate or door, step around a corner, up or down stairs or out from behind a tree. Any natural way of appearing will do.

Now wait patiently and, most importantly, with an open mind as to the appearance of your new friend. He or she will not appear in the guise of anyone you have known in the physical world. Apart from that there are no limits. You may get an alien or a cartoon character. The Guide's appearance will quite possibly have a symbolic value, in which case this will become apparent in your later dealings. It may or may not please you and will not have been chosen for that purpose. Do not be alarmed if you cannot see your Guide's face at first. It will become clear in time. You should feel warmth and approval from your Guide, though. If you sense hostility or feel fear, politely but firmly ask them to leave.

Do not expect too much of yourself or your Guide this first time. Introduce yourself, ask your Guide's name and, if you like, ask one or two open-ended questions such as: 'How can I improve my health?' or 'Is there any advice you want to give me at this time?' Take the first answer that comes, even if it makes little sense to you at the time. When you feel the transaction is complete, express gratitude and take your leave in whatever way seems appropriate. Then return to the physical level in the same manner as in Grounding and Shielding, perhaps taking a little more time than usual.

As soon as you feel firmly located back in your physical body, write down your experiences. These encounters happen on the same plane as dreams and are equally apt to disappear from the waking mind.

Lesson Six

Reversals

These are popular with some readers and not with others. I personally dislike them and have never used them since giving them a brief trial in my student days. There is reason to believe that they are quite a modern innovation. While this is not necessarily damning in itself, in this case it strikes me as the result of someone trying to cover up a weak intuition by having twice as many 'meanings'. As I hope I have shown by now, this kind of approach is very limiting compared to what can be achieved with the Tarot.

For those who wish to try them, reversals either limit or reverse the meaning of the card. Thus, a very positive or negative card becomes less so. A card which is not especially good or bad in itself becomes its opposite. To create reversals, simply cut the cards at some point in the shuffling process and turn half the cards upside down.

The Relationship Spread

The physical shape of this spread should be familiar from Lesson I. We are going to use it in a different way here. This spread can work well for one party in a relationship but really comes into its own when both parties are present. Also, if you and your partner share an interest in Tarot and are open enough with each other, it can be a worthwhile exercise to do a 'spread for ourselves'.

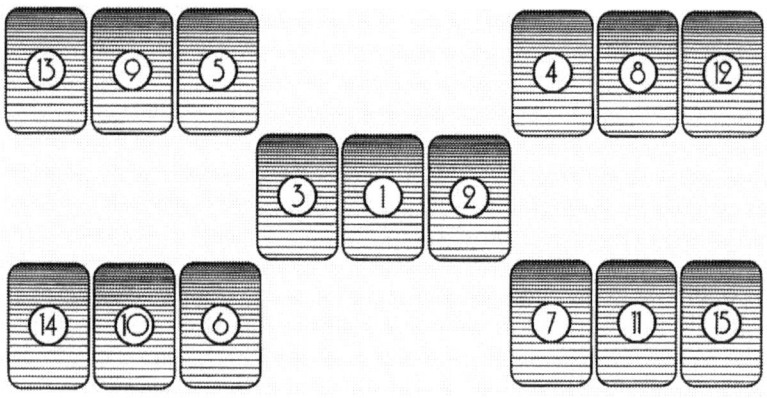

Since we do not know the name or gender of either party in the relationship we can call them A and B for now. Let us suppose A is the one who has asked for a reading. The cards in the two left-hand sections represent factors on A's side. The lower set represents influences from people or circumstances outside the relationship. The upper set represents A's inner thoughts and feelings about it. The right-hand sets do likewise for B. The central set indicates the likely outcome as things stand at present.

Note that there is no 'alternative future' shown explicitly, as there was in the first use of this layout. Often the information given in this spread will make any alternatives and the actions required for them fairly obvious. If more clarification is needed I would suggest following up with a flexible spread like the Mayan, perhaps building the spread around a card from this set that represents what the client wishes to preserve or change.

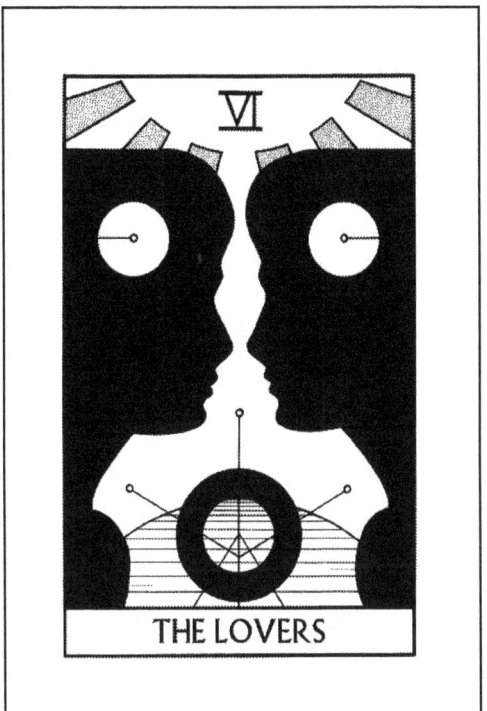

The Lovers

A quick glance at this card suggests an obvious level of meaning, and when the querent's area of concern is romance (which is often) this is indeed a positive card. There is more to it than that, though. The Lovers has relevance to all our relationships, whether with individuals or groups, and to whatever purpose.

The mystics tell us that the Deity divided Itself in order to experience Itself fully. This is a constant among religions and even turns up in secular works such as Breakfast of Champions by Kurt Vonnegut. Whatever else we gain or lose from our meetings with others, we always gain experience.

The Lovers card reminds us that we are parts of the Deity, meeting and interacting with other parts of the Deity. Its astrological attribution, the gregarious and knowledge-hungry sign of Gemini, reminds us that the world is our teacher and every moment of interaction with it a lesson.

The Sixes

With the sixes we come to Tipareth, the second stage point in our journey and the centre of the Tree of Life. This sphere is linked to the Sun, the life-giving warmth at the centre of our little bit of the Galaxy. As you might expect, the sixes have a positive feel.

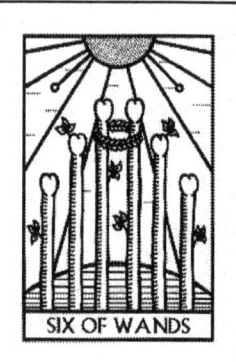

The Six of Wands

Earned success and positive attention. In career matters, sometimes a promotion.

The Six of Cups

Lightness, positivity and good times at the emotional level. This card often shows children at play and speaks of the condition experienced in an ideal childhood. We sometimes forget that it is also the condition of an ideal adulthood. Whether our childhood was ideal or not, it is gone. As adults we can choose to take responsibility for our own happiness or place that responsibility onto others and remain forever unsatisfied.

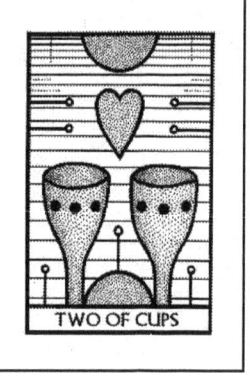

The Six of Swords

Here the emotional tone is neutral. The card refers to travel. If necessary, other cards around it should give an indication of how far and for how long.

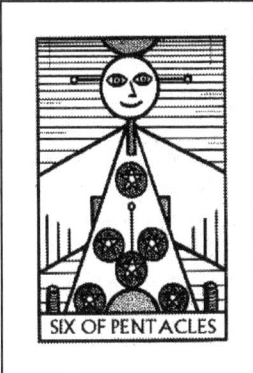

The Six of Pentacles
A positive card for health and money matters. The image of a smiling man handing out money suggests enough abundance that we can afford to be generous.

Exercise VI: Finding The Teachers

Electronics engineers know that the circuit with the least resistance is the most efficient. The same is true of human relationships of all kinds. This exercise is designed to lower our resistance. It is also designed to be an ongoing discipline rather than something to do once and then forget.

For each significant interaction with another person, look for a lesson in the transaction. Then form, and sincerely wish, an appropriate blessing. Of course the latter is easy in the case of positive transactions. It is a little harder in the case of negative ones but still possible. For the driver who cuts you up: 'May you learn better driving habits.' For the grumpy work colleague who offends you with a careless remark: 'May your mood and your manners improve.'

These blessings need not be spoken aloud. In fact it is possible to store them up (making sure to write them down somewhere) and perform the suggested actions in one batch at the end of the day.

Doing this over a sustained period reduces the effect of negative events and makes you more able to conduct your life as you would wish. It also enhances your appreciation of the positive events and makes those who contribute to them more aware of your gratitude, which in turn improves their day.

Lesson Seven

Reading For Yourself

Some people say that you should never read Tarot cards for yourself. This is not usually the silly moral injunction it might appear. There is a genuine and entirely selfish wisdom behind it.

Suppose, for example, I am in a relationship which is in trouble. It appears that my partner does not understand my viewpoint and perhaps never will. I do a reading to find out whether I should try one last time to get through to her or walk away. The cards solemnly advise me that there must be change. This is stating the obvious in the extreme.

Suppose I go to a friend and ask him to read on it, telling him only that the subject is my relationship. After looking at the cards for a long time, he says, 'I don't know how to tell you this but it's time to walk away. From what I can see you'll be happy enough in a short time.' At least I have a definite answer, if at some emotional expense to my friend.

The two examples above are taken from the same life, my own, and the same relationship, which I still enjoy. In the first case I chose to stick it out and won through. In the second I took my friend's advice. It was similar to my own conclusion anyway. I simply wanted to confirm it before taking such a drastic step. Two days after I said my goodbyes, my partner arrived on my doorstep saying, 'Can we talk?' We got the matter sorted in half an hour. I still believe that had I adopted the same attitude as the first time, the result would have been more permanent goodbyes at a later stage.

The point I am making is that reading for yourself is limited by your hopes and fears. By the same logic, reading for a friend or lover can be difficult, as my friend's sadness in the second case illustrates. One way to reduce bias when reading for friends is to have a deck, preferably with quite complex imagery, specifically for that purpose. It is also worth mentioning that on occasion, needing quick answers for myself, I have used the I Ching with great success.

Reading for yourself can be successful in cases where you have no emotional attachment to a specific answer. If my question were, for example, which of several equally promising investments to go for, I would read for myself without hesitation.

The Tree Of Life Spread

Somewhat unusually, this is a spread that lends itself very well to reading for yourself. It takes a highly spiritual perspective, as you might expect from its name, and can be very useful for taking blocked situations up a level in order to fix them. It is my own variation on a fairly well known spread.

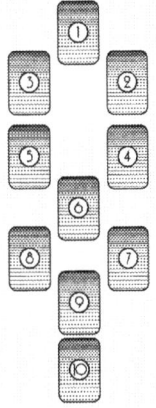

The card positions are read as follows:

1. The current spiritual goal or life lesson.
2. Forces in your favour.
3. Obstacles that cannot be removed and must be circumnavigated.
4. Practical advantages to be gained.
5. Enemies and areas of weakness.
6. Existing knowledge that can be used.
7. Friends and lovers.
8. Knowledge from others.
9. Mental and emotional aspects.
10. The practical issue.

The Chariot

The Chariot is usually shown pulled by two sphinxes, one black, the other white. We have met this colour code before, in the High Priestess, and it has similar significance here. We are reminded that success in life depends on balancing our different qualities and using each where appropriate. The card refers to willpower and determination. Its motto could be 'I can and I will.'

The astrological attribution is Cancer, which may surprise those of you who are used to the rather drippy, passive image given to Cancerians by some popular astrologers. As a Sun- and-Ascendant Cancerian, I have an opinion about this. Cancer is a cardinal sign and will always seek self-determination. Since it is also a water sign, there is a natural ability to perceive and direct emotions. Used well, this shows as charm and empathy. Used badly, it gives the native the appearance of weakness, sulkiness or manipulation. Hence, the challenge for Cancerians is the one illustrated by the Chariot ~ to use all of our energy, and all of the help available to us, in the most appropriate way.

This is also a card of teamwork, especially for those who lead the team, since it is their job to keep all members of the team working together as happily and productively as possible.

The Sevens

Now we start the final part of our journey down the Tree. Since Netzach, the seventh Sephirah, is attributed to Venus, we might expect an easy ride here. Such is not the case. The sevens all show a challenge of one kind or another.

The Seven of Wands

The most common image here is of a fighter in a high position defending himself against six, usually unseen, others. Even though he is outnumbered, his position allows him to control the situation. I see this card as one of acceptable, possibly even enjoyable, challenge.

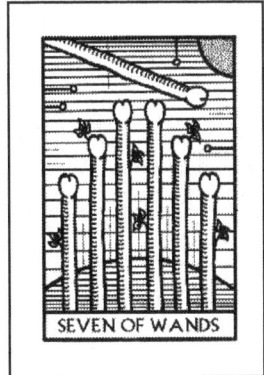

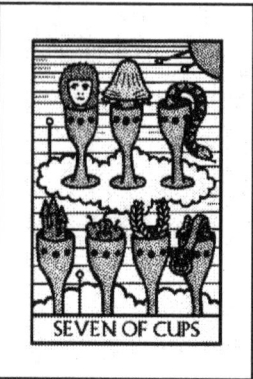

The Seven of Cups
Here the challenge is agreeable, if not necessarily easy. It is that of choice. There may well be no wrong answer to the question.

The Seven of Swords
Here something is being stolen from the querent. This may not be a criminal matter. Often the stolen item is time or emotional or physical energy. Frequently, too, it is with the querent's passive assent. A firmer line could be taken to advantage.

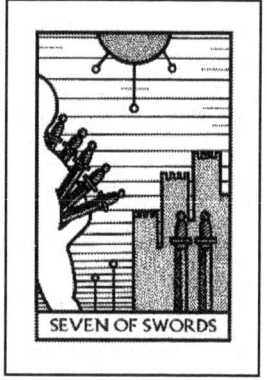

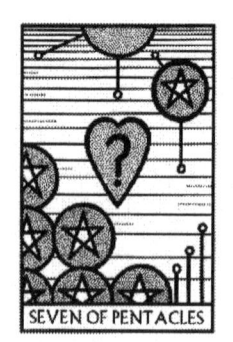

The Seven of Pentacles
Here there is no material lack but the route taken to ensure material security has produced boredom and frustration. It is time to move closer to the heart's desire, even if this means a gamble at the material level.

Exercise VII: Who's Pulling Your Strings?

In Lesson 0 I made brief mention of psychic vampirism. This problem is far more common than the sinister hexes of popular fiction. Fortunately it is also easier to deal with. Grounding and Shielding will take care of new stuff but established links can be more problematic and need a special effort to sever the link.

These links connect via our chakras, the subtle energy gateways in the etheric body that we work on in Grounding and Shielding. This time we will be working from the Crown down to the Root. You may want to begin by doing the Grounding and Shielding, keeping your eyes closed at the end. This serves the purpose of creating a special space around you and an appropriate state of mind for observing the links.

The crown chakra is located, as its name suggests, at the top of the head. You could visualise it as a lotus flower, perhaps making it the same violet colour as used in Grounding and Shielding. When you have that clear, try to notice any cords coming from this chakra. Do not worry about where they come from or go to; all such cords are extraneous to requirements. Mentally cut them.

Now move on to the third eye chakra in the middle of the forehead. Once again, visualising it as a flower. Look for cords and cut any that you find there.

The throat chakra is at the base of the throat. The heart chakra is level with the heart in the middle of the body. The solar plexus chakra is at the base of the ribcage. The sacral chakra is between the navel and the gonads and the base chakra is at the base of the spine. The procedure is the same with all of them. Remember, cutting these cords harms nobody and is likely to improve any relationships you wish to maintain.

You may well notice improvement in your energy level even after doing this once. I would certainly recommend doing it a few days in succession, until you cannot find any cords. It would be wise to repeat it once a month or so thereafter. Not only does it prevent psychic vampirism, it also reduces others' influence over your thoughts and actions.

Lesson Eight

A Question Of Numbers

Some of you may be very puzzled at this point. I have placed the Strength card in this lesson and given it the number 8, while many authorities give that number to Justice and 11 to Strength. Why, you might quite reasonably ask, does this inconsistency occur?

If you look at the sequence of the Zodiac, the order I have used here makes sense. Strength in most decks shows a lion as a major part of the picture. Justice shows a set of scales. Leo and Libra are the obvious attributions. The rest of the signs appear in their accustomed order. Why should these two be different?

Eliphas Levi was the first on record with the transposed sequence. He gives no explanation for it. One theory I have heard, which strikes me as plausible, is that he was trying to honour the form rather than the substance of an oath of secrecy by incorporating a deliberate error in his work. Trust a Roman Catholic priest to come up with this one!

Another explanation, devised by Aleister Crowley, transposes The Emperor and The Star as well. This follows a line in The Book of the Law, a work channelled by Crowley and upon which much of his own work is based, which states 'All these old letters of my Book are aright; but Tzaddi is not the Star.'

Fortunately, for our present purpose, it hardly matters what numbers are attached to the cards. Early Tarot decks do not even show numbers on the Major Arcana. I have chosen the order which strikes me as most logical for teaching purposes. If you choose to get deeply enmeshed in the mysteries of Kabbalistic numerology, it is your affair. In terms of reading the cards, the question is largely meaningless.

The Not Really A Spread At All Spread

This is more a thinking tool than a spread for divination. It evolved when I rang a friend one day and asked how she was. She said, 'I have a whole bunch of problems and I don't know which to try to sort out first. It feels as if, once I get one of them fixed, the rest should sort themselves out.'

I decided to experiment. I asked her to describe the problems one by one and selected a card to represent each one. Then I laid the cards out in a circle and looked at them as if they were a spread created in the usual way, looking for the weakest link. We found it, and my friend got her problems sorted out in days.

Since then I have used the same technique several times, sometimes after a reading and sometimes on its own. It is not a spread in the usual sense but it certainly does a similar job and is a valid way of using the cards to solve problems. Sometimes the problems have not been interconnected in an obvious way, as was the case that first time. The 'domino effect' still seems to work. Once you topple one, the rest follow quickly.

Strength

This is a complex card and can be interpreted in several different ways. Crowley retitles it Lust, expanding on this elsewhere as 'the joy of strength exercised'. This seems entirely reasonable, especially when we consider that the word 'lust' used to be much more broad ranging than simple sexual desire.

My own take is a little different, based on the astrological attribution, Leo. Mrs. Prospero happens to be a Leo, and a pretty typical one at that. Whatever she is, she is absolutely. No holds barred, no turning back, no quarter asked or given. This, to me, is the essence of the card. Decision, action and total commitment.

The Eights

With the eights, we enter Hod, the Sephirah linked to Mercury. Here the Fire and Water suits show the fact of Mercurial change, while Air shows the peril of its absence and Earth shows the value of long-term thinking.

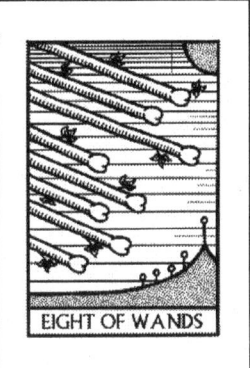

The Eight of Wands

'Expect the unexpected' might be the motto for this card. In itself, it is neither good nor bad. It tells us little of what is to come, except that it will happen rapidly.

The Eight of Cups

A change of heart is shown. Once again, this card is neither positive nor negative in itself, though changes of this order usually give us perspective, at the least.

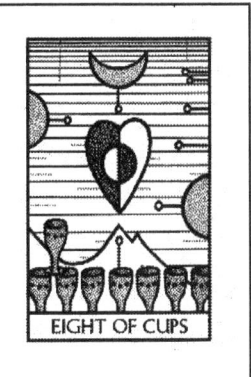

The Eight of Swords

Restriction and difficulty. A change is urgently required but may not be possible, for a time at least.

The Eight of Pentacles
Solid work to long-term advantage. This is not necessarily as dull as it sounds, but it does require persistence.

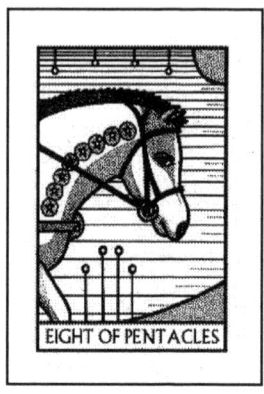

Exercise VIII: Finding Your Strengths
This exercise is about diversification. As Robert Anton Wilson has remarked, specialisation is for insects. When we take up a new activity we stretch ourselves and are apt to make gains in areas other than the new skill.

The exercise is to take up a new activity as different from your present range as possible while still having meaning for you. The only rules are that it must have a physical element and an element of skill. If you love listening to music, for example, but have not taken up an instrument, this would be an ideal time to do so. If your life is fairly sedentary, perhaps a sport of some kind would suit.

Remember, nobody is asking you to reach for international fame and fortune. It is having fun in a new way that counts here. Also, do not let age be a barrier. This exercise was partly inspired by my recently taking up the clarinet. At the time an acquaintance remarked, 'What's the point in that? You're too old to get any good at it.' A week later I found out that my favourite saxophonist took up the instrument at thirty-five, just three years younger than I am now.

Lesson Nine

Tarot As A Memory Aid

Until the advent of the printing press books were extremely expensive and literacy rare. Our ancestors had ways of getting around this problem, the main one being the art or science of Mnemonics, which is still used today. A simple example would be the phrase 'Richard Of York Gave Battle In Vain', which I remember being taught as a child as a way of remembering the colours of the rainbow. There were many more complex examples and one theory about the origin of the Tarot is that it was one of these memory systems. This seems plausible when we consider how popular these systems were among scholars during the Renaissance. The images of early Tarot decks seem to have much in common with those shown or mentioned in the works of Lull, Bruno, Dee and other experts on the subject.

This is, of course, of limited use to the modern reader but there is a way of using the Tarot as a memory aid in modern life. Simply by remembering the images of the pip cards we can construct a grid of 'pigeon holes', as it were, into which we can put up to ten thousand chosen objects. Taking the tens in this instance as zeros, we can arbitrarily call the Wands units, the Cups tens, the Swords hundreds and the Pentacles thousands. (It is of course equally valid to do this the other way around.) Since no zero of thousands will be needed we can give the Ten of Pentacles the number 10,000.

Now we combine images to produce each number as required. For 3057, for example, we have the Three of Pentacles, the Ten of Swords, the Five of Cups and the Seven of Wands. If you are using the Rider Waite deck or one of its derivatives, which are probably the easiest for this purpose, the Three of Pentacles shows a mason putting the finishing touches to a decorative arch. The Ten of Swords shows a man lying face down with ten swords in his back. The Five of Cups shows three cups spilled and two upright, with a figure brooding over the spilled cups. The Seven of Wands shows a man on high ground fighting unseen opponents. Thus, we could place the figure from the Ten under the arch from the Three, three cups knocked over by his fall while two still stand. A figure in the foreground repels would-be looters with a staff. Into this composite image you could put anything you wish to remember under that number.

On the face of it this sounds rather artificial and silly. Nonetheless I have found this and similar systems useful over the years. It can also have side effects. On occasion I have gone back to the images in which I stored something important and found in addition something I had not put there, a warning or a reminder from my unconscious or some unseen helper. This shows why memory systems fascinated such people as Bruno and Dee and why they are still useful in the age of widespread literacy, cheap printing and pocket computers.

The One Card Spread

Opinion is divided about one-card readings. Some people, including a friend of mine with a deservedly international reputation as a reader, see them as a mockery. Their logic, as I understand it, is that it takes a dynamic interaction between cards before the Tarot comes alive and speaks to us in meaningful sentences.

I half agree with this. Certainly, in most situations, it is advisable to give the cards plenty of room to speak. However, there are occasions when a simple yes or no is sufficient by itself. In these situations it strikes me as perfectly legitimate to pick a single card to answer the question.

This practice is also perfectly legitimate in terms of synchronicity. If the events of a given moment in time have the qualities of that moment in time, as Jung said, and if that fact legitimises Astrology and other forms of divination, a single card chosen at random should be as synchronistic as a dozen or more.

It is also worth noting that the Romans used dice for divination. Some people I have met will flip a coin to make decisions. While Tarot is certainly a complex and beautiful language, it is not necessary to make a long speech every time one is asked a simple question.

The Hermit

It is amazingly difficult to be ourselves these days. How can we hear the 'still, small voice within' when so many outer voices drown it out with their opinions about who we are and ought to be? Yet this is precisely what the Hermit bids us do. The lantern he holds is the light of his own motivation, intuition and reason.

His solution to the problem is clear enough. He has taken himself away from the outer voices to listen to the inner one. Sometimes it can be helpful for us to escape to a place of solitude, or at least a place where nobody thinks they know who we are. Few of us can or should do this forever, though, and the realisations gained on a holiday or a retreat too often dissolve into the background when we return to our daily lives.

The trick, it seems to me, is one of keeping in touch with our feelings. If someone tells you a thing, there will be a feeling in your gut telling you whether or not they speak your truth. If you learn to catch that feeling and live by it you will have learned a great lesson that can inspire and empower your life.

The Hermit's astrological attribution is Virgo, a sign of discrimination and distinctions. A pragmatic earth sign, yet ruled by quick-witted Mercury, Virgo takes care of details and brings them into line with the grand plan.

The Nines

The nines bring us to the last stage post in our journey down the Tree of Life. Yesod is ruled by the Moon, our closest heavenly body and one which has a very direct bearing on affairs here on Earth. What happens there is most directly reflected in the outer world.

The Nine of Wands

This card has a defensive feel. A figure stands in front of a barrier, ready to defend against all comers. I see this card as one of resistance to change.

The Nine of Cups

A lovely, straightforward good news card. Sometimes called the Wish Card, this card speaks of having everything as you would wish it.

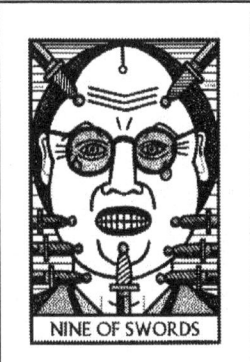

The Nine of Swords

The opposite extreme to the Nine of Cups. Grief and turmoil. There may only be one thing wrong but sometimes one is enough.

The Nine of Pentacles

Plentiful resources. Money and health matters are well starred. A time to attend to other matters or simply to enjoy.

Exercise IX: The Why Game

Part of regaining and maintaining our personal freedom is being aware of our own motivation. Instinct, intuition and 'random' choices certainly have their place but in consciously working towards a goal it is necessary to keep in mind what we want and why. That is what this game is about.

One way to start is to define a current want. This can be something of huge importance, such as 'I want a partner to share my life with', or a relatively trivial thing, such as 'I want a new bicycle'. I would suggest making it the most urgent of your current wants rather than the most important. For example, the life partner may be (and probably should be) vastly more important in the long term, but if your bicycle is your main transport it may have more urgency.

A quick note about positives and negatives here. Try to phrase your wants in a positive fashion. For example, 'I want to own my own home' is much better than 'I want to stop living in crummy rented places'.

Taking the bicycle as an example, the Why game, which is an internal dialogue, might go something like this:

'I want a new bicycle.'
'Why?'
'My old one is very slow.'
'Why?'
'The gears keep sticking in first.'

At this point the Questioner may have a suggestion:

'Why not just replace the gear mechanism?'

Now several things may happen. You may have just hit on a cheaper solution to a problem, which is fine. You may also have a thought such as 'Jenny has a new bike. I want one like hers.' If so, it may be advisable to ask what else Jenny has that you would like. If this yields an answer such as 'quiet confidence' then it is time to look for your own sources of confidence. You could do this by asking questions such as 'When do I feel unconfident?' and then running a Why game on each situation that comes to mind.

It may seem unrealistic to think that a desire for a new bicycle could have such a convoluted origin. Yet we are constantly being told that the right car, the right clothes, the right shaver or whatever will make us smarter, sexier and so much happier. This works because we all have our own associative mechanism. This is neither good nor bad in itself but it can lead to confusion about our goals.

Lastly, never forget the obvious. It might just be that Jenny has a really nice bike.

Lesson Ten

Stasis and Change

If I were seeking to modernise my professional image and appeal to the grey-suit-and-briefcase crowd, I might well change my job title to something like Change Management Consultant. Nearly all clients come to me either to initiate change or to prevent it.

This aspect of the reading dynamic bears further examination. We all have a tendency to think about our own lives from a rather narrow perspective, which is why advice from a friend will often turn up a quick and easy solution to a problem that previously seemed insoluble. Sometimes the reader's role is to show the client what would be blindingly obvious to them if they were not intensely involved in the situation. (It is sometimes possible to do this without knowing what on earth you are talking about, which can be disconcerting at first.)

Preventing change is harder work, generally speaking, than initiating it. The best that can be done in most cases is to direct the energy of change so that the results are more as desired. The type of reading where the client wants to hold things in a fixed pattern can be the most challenging. Their polar opposite is when a client arrives having already started the process and mostly wants reassurance that the right moves have been made. These are easy and fun.

The Kaos Spread

This spread was invented by Andrew Smith, a student of mine, a few months after he finished my course. He was kind enough to share it with me and I include it here with his agreement. It is inspired by Peter Carroll's idea, used in his book *Liber Kaos*, for eight Magickal disciplines denoted by eight different colours.

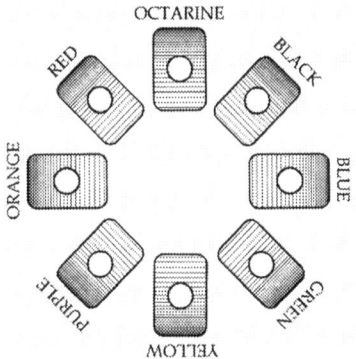

The cards can be read in any order but Andrew points out the natural pairing of opposites within it, a fact which I had not consciously noticed despite reading Liber Kaos several times. The four pairs are:

Black - Purple
Blue - Orange
Green - Red
Yellow - Octarine

The colours are read as follows:

Black	Fears, things or people we need to let go of and leave behind.
Blue	What we create, both for others and ourselves.

Green	Things or people that we attract, for good or ill.
Yellow	Self Image. The way other people see us.
Purple	Hopes and dreams. Things we need to create or bring into our lives.
Orange	What we take from life. Things we cannot self create.
Red	Things or people we resist or drive away, again for good or ill.
Octarine	Our inner Magick. Who we really are.

For those not familiar with the work of Terry Pratchett, Octarine is defined in his novels as the colour of magic, perceived differently by different magic users. Its use in Carroll's work is an interesting example of how a fictional concept can end up having value in the 'real' world.

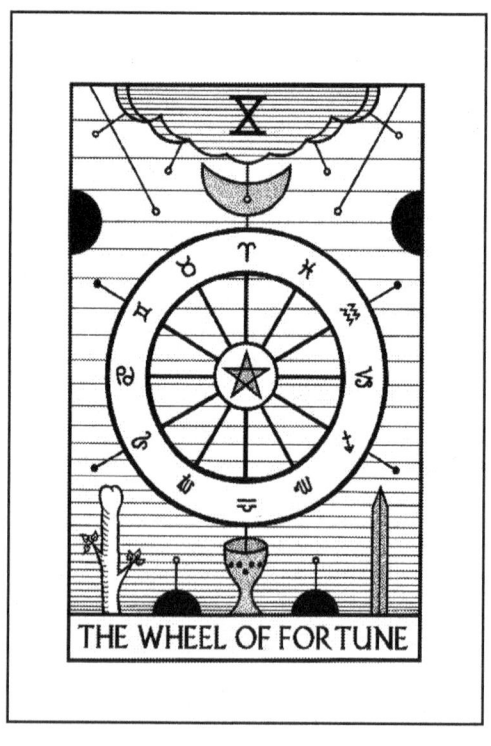

The Wheel of Fortune

The Wheel reminds us that in this Universe change is the only constant. The signs of the zodiac and the four elemental symbols of the Kerubim (man or angel, eagle, lion and bull) are frequently shown in this card, reminding us of the dynamic nature of reality. By accepting this pattern and flowing with it, we gain some measure of control over it. The question changes from 'Shall I change?', which is unrealistic, to 'How shall I change?'

In a reading, The Wheel reminds us to be alert to changing circumstances. What has worked in the past may become redundant and what has failed may now succeed.

The astrological attribution to Jupiter is reminiscent of Shakespeare's words, 'There is a tide in the affairs of men, which, taken at the flood, leads on to fortune.' Time to roll up our sleeves and get to it.

The Tens

The journey started at the aces now comes to its conclusion. As you might expect, the tens all have an extreme quality to them, each according to the nature of its suit.

The Ten of Wands

This card often shows a man carrying a huge and disorderly bundle of staves. From our position as observers, we can see that he could make life easier by tying them together. Sound advice here for the querent. As a friend of mine once put it, 'Don't be lazy, do it the easy way.'

The Ten of Cups

Once again, a lovely, happy card. Especially good for family or group concerns. I often see this card following a negative set and representing the patching up of quarrels.

The Ten of Swords

Backstabbing and deceit. Strangely, this card can offer more hope than the three or the nine, since an alert ear can detect a lie (or an alert mind check its facts) and thus avoid disaster.

The Ten of Pentacles

Health, prosperity and all good things. This card reaches further than its mundane significance and, once again, has a special significance for groups, be it a couple, an extended family or a working group. A suitable place to conclude our journey through the pip cards.

Exercise X: Talking To Aliens

It is difficult to take much interest in New Age thought without sooner or later coming across channelled material. The quality of this material is as varied as its alleged sources. A recent encounter with some of this material, supposedly from entities living in a distant star system, inspired this exercise.

Imagine that you are in communication with a being living on a distant planet. Try to explain to this being some of the fundamentals of human society. Remember to take nothing for granted. For example, how would you explain the role of gender in human societies to a member of a hermaphroditic species?

If you find the above too much of a stretch at first, or if you simply prefer this method, you might try explaining our current society to a visitor from the past. If you do this with enough historical awareness, the resulting view of our progress may surprise you.

Lesson Eleven

Ethics

As with so many areas in Tarot, there is no single authentic voice on ethics for readers. I offer my own set here as a basis on which to work until you find your own.

I will always maintain absolute confidentiality unless its maintenance contributes to extreme harm. (Obviously this wording requires some common sense in the definition of extreme harm. In practice, however, I have yet to find it necessary to break confidentiality.)

I will always make sure, to the best of my ability, that when I make myself available for readings I am in a fit state to do them. To me this means being free of all mind-altering substances, including alcohol, reasonably rested and free of all but fairly trivial levels of physical pain. If you are a beginner, I suggest you also avoid reading when emotionally upset or after a heavy meal. When reading for friends or family, emotional bias can also be a factor.

I will always tell the client what I see in the cards, whether I judge it to be good, bad or indifferent. (Who am I to judge? A divorce, a redundancy, perhaps even a death could be an essential part of a process which brings good things to the client.)

I will not read for people when I consider it would be a waste of their time and money. This includes occasions when potential clients are very drunk or visibly drugged. It can also include 'Tarot addicts' who come to a reader with the same issue over and over again or who would have readings too often for their own good.

If I feel that a reading is not connecting, I will admit to it and take action to remedy it. If this action is unsuccessful, I will decline to take money for my work and make it clear that the failure does not mean that something awful is going to happen. If possible, I will recommend another reader.

While I will cheerfully give relevant advice from my knowledge in other areas, I will always make a clear distinction between that and the content of the reading itself.

I will not take unfair advantage of information given to me as part of a reading. (Once again, this is one I have never had to invoke. It might apply, say, if I were single and found out that a lady I liked was having relationship problems. In this event, I would either admit bias or consider the lady off limits until the matter resolved itself.)

One ethical grey area is reading for children. Speaking personally, I have occasionally read for teenagers, though not for money. In my experience, teenagers who ask for a reading usually have genuine issues which they are ready to address in a serious fashion. The habit in this society of trivialising young people is, in my view, one of the most damaging social ills. Having said that, there may be youngsters (and there will certainly be 'adults') who come to mock or waste your time. The only advice I can give is to judge each case on its merits. As a precaution, I suggest that if you read for children at all you make sure of parental approval. Depending on your location, there may also be legal considerations.

Ultimately I believe that good Tarot ethics derive from a very simple principle. Our aim, like that of good doctors or counsellors, should be to empower our clients and increase their freedom of choice. Actions which further that aim or are neutral to it are ethical. Actions which go against it are not.

The Diamond Spread

This can be a challenging spread for a beginner but is well worth mastering. I used it as my main spread for some years and produced some very memorable readings with it. Its strength lies in its freeform quality, allowing the cards to tell a complex story in their own way.

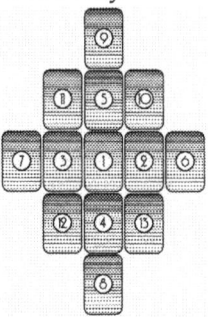

The only structural element, apart from the shape of the spread, is the timeline. This runs from left to right, the centre line being the present. Having said that, the way the spread works in practice often leads to sections forming vertically or in quadrants. The central card often also has great importance.

Justice

The title and image on this card suggest legal matters and certainly that is one level of its meaning. As with the rest of the Major Arcana, though, there is a deeper level of meaning which gives rise to the others. In this case it is the principle of balance. Crowley retitles the card 'Adjustment' and when I see it I know I can expect the client's life to be adjusted in a positive direction.

This principle also holds true at the inner level. When the card turns up in ways which talk about the personality, it refers to the sense of what is right. This is not necessarily a moral issue; it applies equally well to the intuitive aspects of practical work (setting up a carburettor, for example) or to aesthetics (art, cookery, fashion). The key is that in these matters we need to judge something rather than simply use a logical, 'off-the-shelf' answer.

The scales indicate the card's astrological link to Libra. This is a cardinal sign and Librans are often good leaders but they achieve much by charm and by fine-tuning rather than drastic action. The rulership of Venus gives aesthetic sense and a desire to work for the good of all. Curiously, this is a sign noted for producing great generals. This seems like a contradiction until you consider the nature of military leadership. There is truly an 'art of war' and even in the greatest conflicts, intelligence and intuition in balance can win against the odds.

The Court Cards

The classic interpretation of court cards is that they represent people. There are various systems for defining what sort of people in each case. If you are content with a very shallow interpretation that simply gives the person's gender, star sign or age or a few physical details, this is fine.

However, there is a great deal more you can get from the court cards by giving your intuition free rein. A pair of readings I did a few years ago illustrates the point nicely. The first was for a friend who was considering a major business commitment. The King of Cups came up to represent his potential partner in the deal. Looking at the face on the card, trying to sense the man's character and attitude, I got a cynical user, someone who saw two kinds of people ~ winners and losers. He had to win and would cheerfully do so at my friend's expense.

The next reading I did, using the same deck, was for a young lady and it was about a romantic situation. Once again the King of Cups appeared, representing the lady's new partner. Using the same approach, I 'moved in' and was bowled over with the warmth and positivity of the man's feelings for her.

Another level of meaning for the court cards is an indicator of the level of completion of a project or a person's level of development in the area represented by the suit. This is not easy to describe in the abstract (which perhaps is why I have never seen it in print) but hopefully the descriptions in this and the next three lessons should make the concept clear.

With the court cards even more than elsewhere, you should bear in mind that my given meanings are no more than a starting point for your own exploration. Your own feelings about each card should be given more weight than anything you read here or elsewhere.

The Pages

Where they represent people, the Pages do double duty, representing both young women and children. (This assumes the traditional naming of the court cards. As I mentioned before, if a deck uses the more modern convention, whereby the Knights become Princes and the Pages Princesses, I would divide children by gender. Despite being a traditionalist by nature, I rather prefer this arrangement.)

Where they represent events, I see the Pages as beginnings. The difference between a Page and an Ace in this context is that an Ace guarantees a successful outcome, while a Page requires something extra to produce success. The 'something extra' may be intelligence, courage, skill or simple hard work, but it is never beyond the bounds of what the querent can supply. Whether they wish to do so may be another matter.

As a measure of the querent's level of development, a Page indicates that the querent has hardly scratched the surface of his or her potential. When using court cards in this way, it is important to note that the measurement is in relation to individual potential, not to the collective average. Thus, a Page of Swords, for example, may apply to a college graduate.

The Page of Wands

Traditionally, a young woman or child of a fire sign (Aries, Leo or Sagittarius). I see this card as being about temperament; this person speaks their mind directly and honestly, whether it is wise or not. A high-energy person who can be the life and soul of the party or the centre of a destructive whirlwind.

In terms of events, I see this as a change at work. Whether it is a change for better or worse depends on the surrounding cards and the querent's own actions.

As a level of development, I see this as someone who is just starting out in a career or has barely scratched the surface of his or her potential. This may not be their fault ~ there may have been no choice so far ~ but if it comes up in this way you can bet there is a choice now or soon.

The Page of Cups

Traditionally, a young woman or child of a water sign (Cancer, Scorpio or Pisces). The temperament here is gentle and sensitive, often highly creative and with a strong desire to please. These people are often badly hurt by others, yet they never become entirely cynical and can develop excep-

tionally deep relationships when the other party matches their own level of integrity.

As an event, I see this card as the beginning of a love affair or creative project. It does not have the guarantee of success implied by the Ace and I would look to other cards around it to find out whether or not it was worthwhile.

As a level of development I see this card as representing either someone who has concentrated on practical goals at the expense of their emotions or someone who has retained their vulnerability and love of people by conscious choice, sometimes at great cost.

The Page of Swords

Traditionally, a young woman or child of an air sign (Libra, Aquarius or Gemini). The temperament is bookish and logical, often sensitive to slights and with a reserve in social life, which can easily be mistaken for snobbery or standoffishness. These people are often fond of solitude but may end up with more of it than they really want.

As an event, I see this as the start of a new intellectual effort, whether learning, teaching or research.

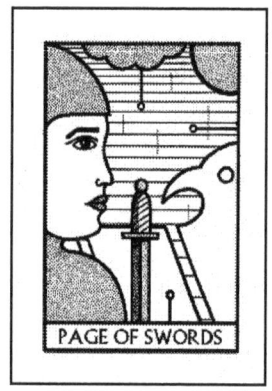

As a level of development this card shows a person whose intellectual accomplishments lie far behind their potential. It usually turns up when there is an opportunity to redress this balance.

The Page of Pentacles

Traditionally, a young woman or child of an earth sign (Capricorn, Taurus or Virgo). I see these people as practical and loyal, though sometimes prone to excessive worry about money and/or health.

As an event, sometimes a move and sometimes a rearrangement in financial affairs.

As a level of development, this card seems to come up for those who have accepted being 'bad at money' rather than learning to handle their finances efficiently.

Exercise XI: Disarming The Enemy

We have talked about some of the negative things human beings can unconsciously or thoughtlessly do to each other and how you can counter the effects of these actions. However, there is one technique that can be very useful in dealing with open hostility.

Suppose, for example, your boss is on the warpath. He calls you into his office and you know what to expect from his tone of voice. Mentally surround him with a pink mist. Pink is the colour of love and can quickly take the heat out of the situation.

Of course this technique will not change the facts that caused the situation. If you have acted foolishly or maliciously you will still have to face the consequences. What the pink mist does is to allow positivity to resurface. If you are being blamed for something that is not your fault it may give you the space you need to point this out. If it is your fault but the other party's reaction is out of proportion then it allows you to restore a balance. The flip side is that it also requires you to act in a civilised fashion.

Lesson Twelve

Dealing With Sceptics

The people I am calling 'sceptics' here fall into three categories, each of whom calls for a different approach.

Those who are most in line with the dictionary definition of the word are open to fresh viewpoints. They are genuinely undecided on whether Tarot and other psychic phenomena are real or not. In these cases, sincerity and careful use of words can make an excellent impression. If they sit down for a reading they are usually very easy to work with since they have little or no emotional resistance to the process.

The second category, what we might call the 'die-hard sceptics', have a belief system that precludes any possibility that psychic phenomena are real and valuable. This may be one of the more rigid varieties of Christianity or an equally rigid faith in atheist materialism. From their perspective, anyone who uses Tarot cards is either a fool or a fraud. Unless they amuse you, I would suggest terminating any conversation with these people as quickly as possible. Their beliefs are too deeply held to make a conversion likely. The emotions surrounding those beliefs can lead to abusive or even violent behaviour.

The third variety of sceptics are not questioning the value of Tarot per se, but your skill as a reader. Their questions are usually polite and reasonable and it is worth taking the time to give them honest answers. Many of my regular clients started out by asking me about my skills and attitude to what I do. Since there is no recognised qualification for readers, intelligent inquiry is the only means these people have of assessing whether or not to give you their time and, if applicable, their money.

The Chakras Spread

This spread is somewhere between the Ba Gua or Houses and the 15-Card Romany in terms of its dynamic in practice. It is also quite time-consuming. It is of course possible to use one card for each chakra but this version gives a very full reading, not just touching each area but giving it a decent look. The format chosen here is adapted to the fact that most readers will want to be closer to the client than the more obvious vertical arrangement would allow. If you feel strongly that a vertical arrangement is necessary, consider having your client sit beside you rather than across the table.

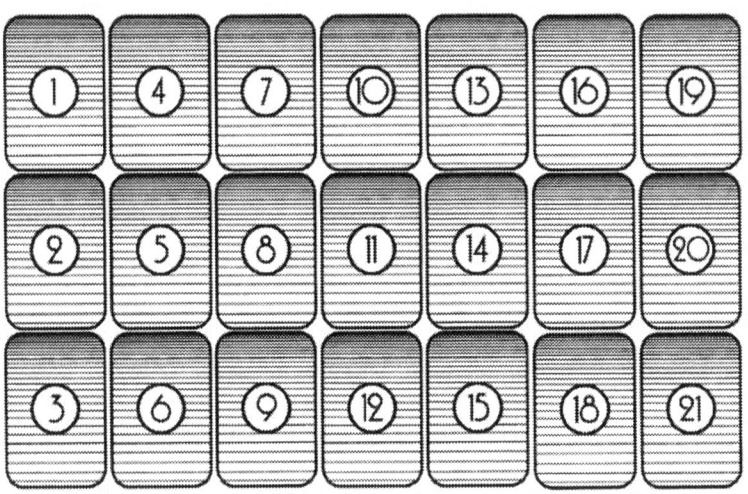

The first three cards deal with the Root Chakra and with personal survival issues.

The second set deals with the Sacral Chakra and with sexuality and moment-to-moment emotions.

The third set deals with the Navel Chakra and with personal energy. Look here particularly for answers to expressed blocks.

The fourth set deals with the Heart Chakra, love (in the broadest sense of the word) and long-term emotions.

The fifth set deals with the Throat Chakra and communication. Again, it can be useful to look for blocks here.

The sixth set deals with the Third Eye Chakra, imagination and psychic ability.

The seventh set deals with the Crown Chakra, spiritual values and the connection to Higher Self.

The Hanged Man

This is the first card we will look at which has a spooky reputation outside of Tarot reading circles. Certainly the title does it no favours, though the image is often more benign. The man is usually hanging by one foot, not from a gallows but from a T-shaped frame. His hands are behind his back and his free leg is crossed behind the other. The face is usually calm and placid.

This card is sometimes referred to as Odin sacrificing Himself to Himself in an effort to gain the Runes. (I have also heard an Odinist of some standing deny this connection but I mention it here because as an analogy for Tarot readers it works well.) I have also heard it mentioned in terms of a Yogic practice of meditating upside down. In either case the significance is the same; something lost and something gained.

There is always some element of sacrifice involved when this card turns up. The key aspect here is that it is voluntary sacrifice, not the painful involuntary loss which has loomed

so large in its fictional 'meanings'. The Hanged Man states a price but he is no foot-in-the-door hard salesman. We buy or not as we please.

His astrological attribution is Water, the emotional element. Emotions are the deciding factor in so many of the bargains we strike in our lives, whether the exchange is financial, emotional, spiritual, sexual, intellectual or creative. Water is also something which flows in and out of our lives. Its movement, both to and from us, gives it its value.

The Knights

Where they represent people, the Knights do a simpler job than the pages, representing young men. How young is young? A quick survey of my bookshelf gives me thirty, thirty-five and forty as the borderline. I suppose the only honest answer is 'young is as young does'. I find that the age distinction varies according to the age of the questioner.

As an event, the Knights show a project half completed. Though success is not yet guaranteed, there is more assurance than with the Pages. Luck is no longer seen as the major factor in the equation.

As a measure of development, the Knights are again a halfway stage. It is worth pointing out, though, that the second half is often an easier ride than the first. Age has its compensations.

The Knight of Wands

Traditionally, a young man of a fire sign (Aries, Leo or Sagittarius). I see this young man as a 'go-getter' with a strong self-image, though not necessarily an excessive ego. He wants the best for himself at all levels and is willing to put the hours in to make it so.

As an event, a step forward in the career area, usually without a change of employer unless the career is one in which short-term employment is the norm.

As a level of development, either a change in attitude from 'I should be given' to 'I can get' or a change in outer circumstances which removes a block.

The Knight of Cups

Traditionally, a young man of a water sign (Cancer, Scorpio or Pisces). To me this man has qualities I would associate strongly with my fellow motorcyclists. He is emotionally open, yet curiously self-reliant and almost impossible to knock off centre. He also tends to be well travelled, which accounts for at least some of these qualities.

As an event, a step forward or a stablisation in a relationship or a creative project.

As an indicator of emotional development, a halfway stage. Whether this represents fast or slow progress is a matter of opinion and probably best left without comment in any case.

The Knight of Swords

Traditionally, a young man of an air sign (Libra, Aquarius or Gemini). This man always comes across to me as reserved and bookish, often someone who has difficulties socially and almost always someone who resists socialising for its own sake.

As an event, a step forward intellectually. If this is a new venture, it is in an area where there is already some knowledge.

As a stage in development, this card indicates room for further progress. This needs to be stated carefully to avoid insult. Be aware that the progress may be broadening rather than deepening knowledge.

The Knight of Pentacles

Traditionally, a young man of an earth sign (Capricorn, Taurus or Virgo). I see this as someone with strongly developed practical skills and a strong physicality. Often highly intelligent but with a distaste for academic environments.

As an event, a stablisation of either health or money issues.

As a stage of development, this is an indicator of growing awareness of the practical issues in life, mainly those of health and money.

Exercise XII: Affirmations (With A Twist)

You may have come across the concept of affirmations before. The normal procedure is to speak or write a repeated statement that something is as you wish it to be. An example would be 'I have the money for all the things I want.' This is an adaptation that can be useful for goals you consider too big for the manifestation method in Lesson I.

For our purposes it will be sufficient to repeat your statement mentally. Keep a notebook and pen handy, though, and be alert for any thoughts that crop up between repetitions. Even if these thoughts seem to have nothing to do with your affirmation, write them down.

You could repeat the statement a fixed number of times or for a fixed period of time. I would suggest the latter as a fixed number of times requires a counting device such as a rosary to avoid giving too much attention to the counting process.

When you finish, review your list of interruptions. Some will be directly relevant, such as a thought that if you had more money you would eat out more often. Others may seem at first to have no relevance, such as the thought 'I must call Fred today.' In this case I would look first at what Fred represents at a basic level. Does he work for an organisation that could help you to earn more or to make your money go further? Is he someone you could work with? Has he said something recently that might be useful? Then I would look at Fred symbolically. Is he someone who always seems to have cash in his pocket, or who never does?

We are looking for several things here. One is any clue as to how you can move nearer to the desired goal. The other is any inner resistance to that goal. (Does Fred have lots of money and drink too much? Are you afraid you would do so if you had the money?)

It may be worth doing several sessions on this, perhaps ten minutes a day for a week. This should unearth most of your resistance and may throw up some useful ideas for achieving your goal at a practical level.

Lesson Thirteen

A Look At Correspondences

We have already looked at the correspondences between Tarot and Astrology and, to a lesser extent, those between Tarot and the Tree of Life. Equally valid correspondences exist with various mythologies and with such things as perfumes, trees and animals. In fact it is possible to connect Tarot cards with practically anything.

Aleister Crowley was one of the greatest experts on correspondences and Liber 777, his extended Table of Correspondences, is still regarded as authoritative and widely used more than half a century after his death. Magickal ritual is obviously the primary reason he was interested in these matters but, for those who enjoy mythology, a browse through his tables can be quite illuminating.

There is a danger of seeing things as too closely linked so that we lose some of the subtleties. The Lovers card, for example, is not the same thing as the Astrological sign Gemini. They share some characteristics and have roughly similar roles in their respective systems. To claim more than that for their connection is to start to lose the value of both.

The Annual Forecast Spread

This spread is ideal for those clients who like to get an annual checkup with a Tarot reader in the same way one might with a doctor or dentist. The dynamic is very simple - a card for each month, starting with Card 1 as the month from the time of the reading. One can, of course, run extensions on any months that look particularly interesting.

Death

Prepared by our encounter with the Hanged Man, we now come to the most blatantly negative image in the Major Arcana. The skeletal figure, complete with scythe and black cloak, often mounted on a white horse, seems to have an all-too-obvious meaning. The number 13 at the top of the card seems to reinforce it. Thankfully for aspiring readers, this assumption is even more wrong here than before.

The Death card stands for radical changes in the querent's life. These will usually be outwardly visible changes. Getting married or divorced, having a child (especially the first), changing profession and moving house are all typical events signified by this card.

If this seems odd, consider what happens when, for example, you become a parent. A new life brings with it new responsibilities. There will be changes in your social life, your daily routine, your financial priorities. Old friends may distance themselves and new ones appear. In short, you will be reinventing yourself ~ 'dying' and being 'reborn'. The step is also irreversible; short of immense personal tragedy, there is no such thing as an ex-parent.

Astrologically, the card links to Scorpio, a sign which has intense emotions and a penchant for sudden, dramatic changes at long intervals.

The Queens

Following our scheme, the Queens represent mature women. The age distinction here is, if anything, a little subtler than with men. There are sometimes less clear signals of a woman's age in her physical appearance and outward status than for a man. In either case, the old definitions of 'right' ages at which to do things are thankfully going out of the window.

As an event, the Queens represent something nearing its completion. There is still time for a late effort to change details if necessary and careful attention may still be needed for the desired outcome but the end is in sight.

As a measure of development, the Queens again represent near-completion. The querent has now learned most of the major lessons for this lifetime in the area specified by the card concerned. Queens often come up in this capacity when a querent is ready for his or her 'finals', as it were. This will be a major event, in the area of life specified by the Queen, which gives greater definition to the querent's life henceforth and allows increased growth in other areas.

The Queen of Wands

Traditionally, a mature woman of a fire sign (Aries, Leo or Sagittarius). I see this woman as strong-willed and energetic with a clear idea of where she wants to go. As a friend she can be a very dynamic influence, though her own ability to withstand hard verbal knocks may cause her to be less than gentle and seem somewhat domineering. As an enemy she will be utterly ruthless but fair in the sense that she moves directly and honestly.

As an event, this Queen represents significant progress in the career area.

As a stage of development, she indicates a learning or an integration in the career area which allows further progress.

The Queen of Cups

Traditionally, a mature woman of a water sign (Cancer, Scorpio or Pisces). To me this woman is often quiet, reflective and creative. She is often a good listener, but when she herself needs some loving care she may find it difficult to ask for it.

As an event, this card shows a major lesson learned, a 'rite of passage', at the emotional level.

As a stage of development, she shows a high level of understanding of emotional dynamics and possibly a strongly developed creative aspect to the querent's character.

The Queen of Swords

Traditionally, a mature woman of an air sign (Libra, Aquarius or Gemini). Once again, I see this woman as reserved ~ she is happy enough in her own company. Always intelligent and usually educated, she can seem aloof or snobbish, though she herself would not see her behaviour in those terms. Sometimes this card turns up to indicate an elderly woman.

As an event, this card shows the start or completion of a stage of formal learning, not necessarily academic but always requiring intelligence and activating it in a powerful way.

As a stage of development, this card shows someone who has done most of the required formal learning for his or her current life goals.

The Queen of Pentacles

Traditionally, a mature woman of an earth sign (Capricorn, Taurus or Virgo). I see this woman as practical, trustworthy, perhaps inclined to pessimism. She is always willing to help people fix problems, but can be impatient with those who merely want to vent about them.

As an event, this is a step closer to reaching a practical goal.

As a stage of development, this card shows that the querent has considerable competence at the material level. They may feel otherwise, especially if young, since that competence will have been gained by hard lessons and challenges.

Exercise XIII: Playing with Time

For this exercise, imagine that you know beyond question that you will die in exactly one year from now. You will have a good standard of health until that moment and you are not obliged to tell anyone about your death or make any preparation for it. (We will assume wills and such have already been attended to.) The exercise is to decide what you would do with your time.

When you are done with planning your year, try different timescales. Ten years. A week. Five minutes. See how this changes your perspective and your priorities.

Gurdjieff apparently said that we should have an organ to continually remind us of the date of our own death. I am not sure I agree. It seems to me that we live best when we live each day as if it could be our last, but also as if we may have a hundred more years to live.

Lesson Fourteen

Personal Correspondences

Some authors have suggested that it is a good idea for students of Tarot to try to devise their own correspondences with Astrology, the Tree of Life and various mythologies. This strikes me as an extreme example of reinventing the wheel. Few of us have the scholarly attributes, the leisure or the facilities available to Levi, Mathers or Crowley. The chances of our improving on their systems are therefore minimal.

However, we do all have a unique set of people and circumstances to draw on. Devising correspondences for friends, family and those objects that may represent key factors in our lives can help us to understand Tarot better. It can also help us to have an intuitive understanding of the way that archetypal forces play themselves out in our lives.

As an example, when I first devised this exercise during my first flush of interest in Tarot, I had a friend who was forever pointing out others' faults. He seemed to take a sadistic delight in breaking people down and pointing out their 'illogical' ways of doing things. He was not a happy or successful man himself but was full of cures for others' problems. Since his emphasis was on logic I linked him to the Emperor, a clear example of its negative face.

My current take on the Emperor would be myself, since I feel markedly more in charge of my own destiny and more content with my lot than ever before. The implication is that I have learned to assimilate and use the headstrong energies of that archetype more constructively. It is also noticeable that my present group of friends includes many people who are self-employed, or who in some other way demonstrate self-dependence to an unusual extent, but who do not feel a need to tell others how to run their lives.

The Destination Spread

This is an example of a spread invented in a flippant and playful way that works well in a serious context. I was sitting on a train to London thinking about this book when the train passed Gatwick Airport. I thought 'Why not have a spread in the shape of an aeroplane?' Five minutes later the table in front of me was covered in Tarot cards and a plan and dynamic had emerged.

The spread is designed for reading for yourself, though you could use it for others if they are open to discussing their private thoughts and ideas with you and abandoning conventional ideas of what a Tarot reader does.

Cards 1-4 represent the four elements in traditional Tarot order; Fire, Water, Air, Earth.

Cards 5-7 represent what we need to put out into the world in the near future.

Cards 8-10 represent what we need to be open to receive from the world in the near future.

Cards 11 and 12 represent the outcome or goal.

Temperance
After the rather spooky images on the last two Major Arcana, Temperance presents a welcome relief. The usual image is of an angelic being pouring water from one cup into another. One of his feet is on land, the other in moving water. The contrast of opposites here, with the motion of the water between the cups, brings us back to the theme of balance, approached from a different angle by Justice. It is a key concept, in Tarot as in life. 'Be moderate in all things, including your moderation' was one of my father's favourite sayings, and an apt one to symbolise the meaning of this card.

In practice, I see this card often when somebody has been experiencing strange and unpleasant times and is coming up for a respite. It may suggest a way to get that respite, by modifying habits of thought or action, or simply show that it is on its way.

A development from this meaning is that of healing. To heal is to make whole, to restore a proper working balance. When this card turns up as a character trait I find that the querent is on what I call the Path of the Healer. This usually involves a troubled early life, with complex emotional issues and often money or physical health problems, and learning to play a supportive role to others. Here, it is necessary to apply the term 'healer' somewhat broadly. The querent may exercise this quality as anything from a car mechanic to a diplomat, or decline to use it at work and simply be a good friend to those in need. The key point is that they have suffered, they have learned to make it better and they are motivated to help others to do the same.

The astrological attribution here is Sagittarius, a sign mythologically associated with Chiron, the wounded healer. Sagittarians often demonstrate the quality of 'tough love', being somewhat wearing company when there is room for it but the first to cut out the nonsense and help out when it is required. Being a mutable sign, they make changes very quickly (and perhaps a little ruthlessly) when required.

The Kings

With the Kings we reach the end of the cycle of the court cards. Following our scheme, the Kings represent mature men. Whether the maturity is physical, psychological or both will vary with the individual.

As an event, a King represents successful completion, usually of something reasonably large.

As a measure of development, a King shows that the querent has completed all of the required learning for this lifetime in the area shown by the suit. Obviously, this does not preclude further voluntary learning; it does however indicate that life in the relevant area should be relatively easy henceforth.

The King of Wands

Traditionally, a mature man of a fire sign (Aries, Leo or Sagittarius). To me this man is one who expects to be a leader. Whether this trait shows through positively or negatively obviously depends on circumstances but he is honest as friend or foe, never asking of others what he himself would not give and never stooping to dishonesty for an easy victory.

As an event, this King shows a key stage successfully reached in the career area. It may be a promotion, a change of career or an honourable retirement. To me it always shows a definable step towards the heart's desire in this area.

As a measure of development, this card shows a high degree of competence in the career. Incidentally, here even more than elsewhere, it is important to remember that careers are not purely about doing things that earn money. 'Wife and mother' or 'voluntary worker' can be as true a career as 'brain surgeon' or 'builder'.

The King of Cups

Traditionally, a mature man of a water sign (Cancer, Scorpio or Pisces). To me, perhaps because it is my own significator, this card has a rich collection of faces. Sometimes I see him as a 'woman's man' in the positive sense of a man who likes and understands women, sometimes a 'ladies' man' in the sense of a womaniser. Sometimes he seems understanding of people, other times he seems to retreat from

his sensitivity into cynicism and possibly alcohol or drugs. Sensitivity is the keyword here. Whether it is a blessing or a curse depends upon and shows the measure of the man.

As an event, this card shows the completion of a creative endeavour or the development of a romance into something more committed.

As a level of development, this card shows that someone has developed fully at the emotional level. This development will not have been won without cost and there may well be battle scars.

The King of Swords

Traditionally, a mature man of an air sign (Libra, Aquarius or Gemini). To me this card shows a man who is accomplished intellectually and who thinks more readily than feels. There is often a sadness about this, a more sensitive soul beneath an arid exterior, but others who are smart enough to perceive this aspect of him had best also be smart enough not to comment on it to his face.

As an event, this is the success of an effort at the intellectual level, whether of learning or teaching.

As a measure of development, the card shows a strongly developed intellect, though nobody who has reached this stage will ever cease learning. Why stop when you are having fun?

The King of Pentacles

Traditionally, a mature man of an earth sign (Capricorn, Taurus or Virgo). This card shows me a man who enjoys the finer things in life and the game of getting them. He sees life as a game to be won, but also to be enjoyed. He is generous ~ he can afford to be ~ but never wasteful.

As an event, I see this card simply as material improvement.

As a level of development, this card shows that the querent has learned the main lessons of the material level of life. As with the King of Cups, there may well be scars. Yet these add to the sweetness of the victory. A fine wine tastes even better if it was once a world away.

At this point, at the risk of being tedious, I remind you that what I have said about the court cards is a personal interpretation. One of my favourite Tarot decks, the Cosmic, shows another very personal interpretation of the cards, apparently using film stars as models. The King of Wands, for instance, looks like Sean Connery, while his Queen is the delectable Joan Collins. Approach the court cards through your own intuition. Be playful and they will come alive for you, each playing his or her part in the dance. Try to pin them down and they become one-dimensional.

Exercise XIV: Never Say Never

This is another reading assignment. Go to a bookshop or library and choose a book in a category you would never normally read. If the category is one you have thought of up to now as trashy or mindless, so much the better. In this event I would suggest going to a bookshop that specialises in the type of literature involved and asking for a recommendation. The intention here is to expand your horizons, not to deliberately read rubbish.

If your literary tastes are already omnivorous, try doing the exercise with music. Some of my favourite musical 'finds' have been in categories I would not have chosen for myself. Another category that would work here is movies, especially if you are not a regular moviegoer. I would recommend visiting a cinema, though, rather than renting a video or DVD.

Lesson Fifteen

A Word About Curses

There are those who would have us believe that black Magick is the only kind there is and that if you so much as share a taxi with someone who owns a set of Tarot cards you are asking for trouble. At the other extreme there are those who appear to believe there is no such thing as a 'dark side'. The truth, as you might expect, is somewhere in between.

Curses and hexes are extremely rare, not because they are difficult but because anyone who is mentally focussed enough to use them effectively can usually find a way to get what they want without hurting anybody. Many people believe themselves cursed because of a run of bad luck, perhaps preceded by an argument with someone believed to have 'the power'. The best way to deal with this is to show the person how to raise their own energy level, perhaps through something like the Grounding and Shielding exercise but with a different emphasis.

Another reason why people can feel 'cursed' is that they have too many cords pulling energy from them in the manner discussed in Exercise VIII. This is pretty similar to the leechlike way that some curses work so the mistake is understandable.

Again, the cure is obvious. Teach the person the technique. While the words used in this book are obviously copyright, the practice of decording is too old to be anyone's intellectual property.

A third kind of 'curse' is less common, though still more so than the genuine article. This is when someone who has some potential as a medium makes accidental contact with a spirit, usually a departed human, and allows it to form a connection with them. Often they are unaware that they have the power to deny it access to their consciousness. Telling them this, perhaps accompanied by one or both of the above exercises, is usually enough to fix the problem. If it is not, I would suggest finding a specialist in these matters. Your local New Age shop may well know of one.

Incidentally, if anyone ever announces that they are going to curse you, it is quite safe to assume they would not know how. If you laugh at them they will very likely go away rather than risk further humiliation.

The Horseshoe Spread

This is a traditional spread that I find useful in looking at specific questions. It can be used for a quick take on a situation or as a basis for a more in-depth study.

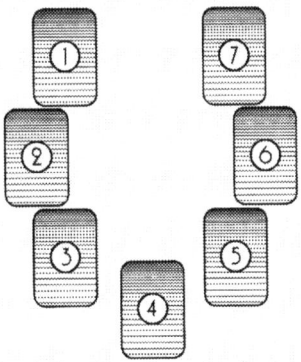

Card 1 shows the past history of the issue, or some relevant aspect of it.
Card 2 shows present circumstances.
Card 3 shows future conditions.

Card 4 shows the best style or course of action for success.
Card 5 shows others' attitudes and opinions.
Card 6 shows obstacles or difficulties.
Card 7 shows the likeliest outcome.

I hope that by now it goes without saying that if the last card shows an undesirable outcome it is possible to lay out extensions or a whole new spread and look for ways to change it.

The Devil

Now we are back among the sinister images with the classic Christian bogeyman. Some modern Pagan interpretations show a more benign image based upon Hearn, the horned hunting god, or another equivalent deity. As we found with Death and the Hanged Man, the image belies a concept which is in itself neither good nor evil.

To understand this card we need to go back to the Mediaeval cosmology. In those times the Devil was seen as a natural and necessary part of the system, a kind of spiritual policeman and judge testing sinners and handing out punishment according to their crimes on a strict but fair basis. He was like a governor in a machine, limiting its power but smoothing its progress and preventing its self-destruction.

Applying this to the human psyche, we soon find something in ourselves which plays the Devil's Advocate, testing our ideas and holding us in check or keeping us at our labours when we feel tired or hopeless. Self-discipline is what we call it when it seems constructive, habit or lack of self-esteem when it appears destructive. Too much of it would leave us crippled by all manner of phobias; too little and we would never complete anything.

The astrological attribution is Capricorn, a Cardinal sign whose primary achievements often come late in life. Typical natives of this sign exhibit the quality we have been talking about here in abundance. They are loyal friends and implacable enemies. They know what they want and can wait, and work, as long as it takes.

Exercise XV: Making It Happen

This exercise is a very simple one on the surface but could get quite complex, depending on how far you choose to take it.

The first step is to go to your favourite news source and find a story that has some meaning for you personally. It could be about international events or a human interest story in the local newspaper. What is important is that it generates some emotion in you.

If it is a big one you may want to research it through several different sources. (This can be quite instructive in itself. Noticing the different 'facts' and emphases in, say, a conservative and a left-wing news source may make you wonder about the validity of what you hear from either.)

Now write a poem or a song about the story. It need not be very long but it needs to fully express your feelings on the matter. Do not stop until you feel you have done this, even if this means doing the exercise in several sittings.

If the story is one with two opposing points of view, you may want to try the additional exercise of writing something from the opposite viewpoint to the one you instinctively side with. Try to genuinely get into the mindset of your opponents rather than writing a pastiche.

Lesson Sixteen

Dealing With 'Bad' News And Crises

If you do a significant number of readings you will eventually have to give somebody what appears to you to be bad news. This can be awkward and uncomfortable even for an experienced reader. Some preparation is needed.

The first thing to recognise is that what seems to you to be bad news may well be nothing of the sort to your client. The end of a relationship, for instance, may be a welcome return to freedom rather than a sad loss. Even a death, under exceptional circumstances, may turn out to be a good thing.

The second thing is that clients are often aware of bad news long before the reading. They may need an outer person to voice that knowledge before they can fully assimilate it. Once they hear it they can begin to heal it. They may also be able to limit its damage by knowing about it in advance.

I am sure you realise by now that the classic horror story situation of a reader seeing a client suffering some horrible fate is exactly that, a thing for stories rather than real life. Why would the fates draw a client to you if they were inextricably doomed to some awful nemesis? Of course, in the unlikely event that you see such an event, telling the client could save a life, or perhaps several.

On a related topic, clients will sometimes be in the middle of a crisis when they ask for a reading. It is a good idea to keep a list of the contact details for any skilled professionals of any kind that you trust. In the course of readings I have been known to give out telephone numbers for accountants and carpenters. On one occasion I believe a client got a job through another client who happened to be a recruitment consultant. Of course it is also worth acquainting yourself with spiritual specialists and any therapists in disciplines you respect.

A Spread For Peace

This spread is designed for use by any two individuals who find themselves in disagreement but have enough good will towards each other to desire a peaceful solution. Its derivation is obviously the symbol used by peace campaigners since 1958. I should point out that my use of it is not intended as a political gesture.

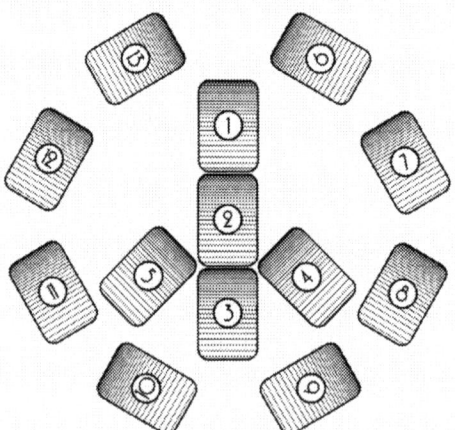

Cards 6-9 and 10-13 represent the initial positions taken by the two parties. Cards 4 and 5 represent the way they present these positions and anything about that which could be changed to advantage. Finally, cards 1-3 represent the solution.

Obviously this spread is a basis for a discussion rather than a reading in the usual sense but it can work well in avoiding unnecessary friction between friends. Sometimes the very act of affirming mutual goodwill is enough to produce a solution.

The Tower

Different artists have given us two seemingly opposite styles for this card. The traditional approach shows a falling tower, usually struck by lightning and showing a crowned man and woman falling beside it. Modern artists often show an intact tower, lit positively and looking strong.

Once again, these seeming contradictions show two faces of the same force. 'Force' is the word here, too. The obvious phallic symbolism suggests the astrological attribution of Mars and the raw power implied. We could perhaps see this as the power which needs to be directed and controlled through the previous card.

Relating this to practical life, we can see a sudden burst of energy for good or ill. It could be utter disaster and/or violence or a turning point from being a victim of circumstance to taking control of our lives. Surrounding cards should indicate which option fits the case. Indeed, the Tower is a good argument against using only the Major Arcana for readings.

Exercise XVI: The Rant

If you have been doing the exercises given up to now you should find that far less of your time and energy is taken up with anger at other people's words or actions. However, we all have a past and most of us have some anger to deal with over past issues or events.

This exercise is a way of dealing with such past-related energy blocks. It can also be adapted to handle present situations in which, for whatever reason, you feel powerless to act.

The first part is to spend a while making a list of past events that still rile you. It does not matter if your present self considers these things silly. What matters is the emotions attached to them. An event is not trivial if it still triggers strong feelings.

Once your list is complete, see if there are any groupings. For example, do many of the events involve your father? We are not attempting psychoanalysis here but defining the people involved for convenience.

Now write a letter about each incident or, where possible, each group of incidents. Make it as furious as you like. There is not the slightest need to be fair to anybody or to mind your language. Put all the emotion you feel onto the paper.

When you think you have finished writing (and I realise this may be something to spread over several days), lay the letter aside for a day or two in a private place. Do this as many times as necessary until no more emotion comes.

Then make a little ritual of burning the paper. This can be as simple as throwing it in the fire, if you are lucky enough to have a real fire, or as elaborate as you like. The important thing is to recognise that you are saying goodbye to the incidents and making room in your psyche for something more useful.

Lesson Seventeen

Astrology And The Tarot

Each of the Major Arcana represents a Planet, Sign or Element, with the Fool, the Hanged Man, the Last Judgment and arguably the World doing double duty to accommodate the outer planets (which were discovered comparatively recently) and Earth (which is also a latecomer to that system). Twelve of the Court Cards represent the twelve Signs of the Zodiac and the pip cards 2-10 represent the Decans (ten-degree sections within each Sign, each with its own planetary rulership).

To add to the fun there are differences of opinion about many of these attributions. Here I have given my own version, which, being based on the Golden Dawn, is probably the commonest in use. Where I give two attributions, the first is the one used by the Golden Dawn and the second is from a post-GD source.

The Fool	Air/Uranus
The Magician	Mercury
The High Priestess	The Moon
The Empress	Venus

The Emperor	Aries
The Hierophant	Taurus
The Lovers	Gemini
The Chariot	Cancer
Strength	Leo
The Hermit	Virgo
The Wheel of Fortune	Jupiter
Justice	Libra
The Hanged Man	Water/Neptune
Death	Scorpio
Temperance	Sagittarius
The Devil	Capricorn
The Tower	Mars
The Star	Aquarius
The Moon	Pisces
The Sun	The Sun
Judgment	Fire/Pluto
The World	Saturn/Earth
King of Wands	Aries
Queen of Wands	Leo
Knight of Wands	Sagittarius
Page of Wands	Fire
King of Swords	Libra
Queen of Swords	Aquarius
Knight of Swords	Gemini
Page of Swords	Air
King of Cups	Cancer
Queen of Cups	Scorpio
Knight of Cups	Pisces
Page of Cups	Water
King of Pentacles	Capricorn
Queen of Pentacles	Taurus
Knight of Pentacles	Virgo
Page of Pentacles	Earth

Ace of Wands	Fire
Two of Wands	Mars in Aries
Three of Wands	Sun in Aries
Four of Wands	Venus in Aries
Five of Wands	Saturn in Leo
Six of Wands	Jupiter in Leo
Seven of Wands	Mars in Leo
Eight of Wands	Mercury in Sagittarius
Nine of Wands	Moon in Sagittarius
Ten of Wands	Saturn in Sagittarius
Ace of Swords	Air
Two of Swords	Moon in Libra
Three of Swords	Saturn in Libra
Four of Swords	Jupiter in Libra
Five of Swords	Venus in Aquarius
Six of Swords	Mercury in Aquarius
Seven of Swords	Moon in Aquarius
Eight of Swords	Jupiter in Gemini
Nine of Swords	Mars in Gemini
Ten of Swords	Sun in Gemini
Ace of Cups	Water
Two of Cups	Venus in Cancer
Three of Cups	Mercury in Cancer
Four of Cups	Moon in Cancer
Five of Cups	Mars in Scorpio
Six of Cups	Sun in Scorpio
Seven of Cups	Venus in Scorpio
Eight of Cups	Saturn in Pisces
Nine of Cups	Jupiter in Pisces
Ten of Cups	Mars in Pisces
Ace of Pentacles	Earth
Two of Pentacles	Jupiter in Capricorn
Three of Pentacles	Mars in Capricorn
Four of Pentacles	Sun in Capricorn
Five of Pentacles	Mercury in Taurus

Six of Pentacles   Moon in Taurus
Seven of Pentacles   Saturn in Taurus
Eight of Pentacles   Sun in Virgo
Nine of Pentacles   Venus in Virgo
Ten of Pentacles   Mercury in Virgo

So now that you have these attributions, what should you do with them? Well, you may be glad to know that there is no need to memorise them at this stage. Indeed, I know of excellent readers with similar levels of experience to myself who still do not know more than one or two of them.

If you already know some Astrology, especially if it is the more traditional kind, you may find it useful to examine these attributions and see what they add to your appreciation of the cards. (This process may also add to your understanding of Astrology.)

Another use for these attributions is timing. Suppose, for example, I want to move and have found a place but am seeking some idea of when the paperwork will go through. I shuffle and pull a card and it is the Nine of Swords. Normally this is not a good card but there is no question of good or bad here; the question is purely one of time. This card gives me the middle Decan of Gemini, approximately 3-12 June. If I had thought to do a reading of this kind prior to my last move it might have saved me a lot of worry. I made an offer on a flat in February and eventually moved on 11 June.

The Planetary Spread

This is a simple and traditional spread that works well in situations where a fair amount of detail is needed but there is not time for a larger spread. Used as a general spread it works like this.

The Moon - Home life
Mercury - Business and communication
Venus - Love and relationships
Sun - Personal goals and achievements
Mars - Difficulties and hostilities
Jupiter - Gain and expansion
Saturn - Restrictions and limits

The Star

Our journey now takes us into calmer waters. The Star usually shows a young naked woman pouring water from an urn or otherwise handling water at a riverbank. Above her in a starry sky, one star shines brighter than the rest and illuminates the scene.

To me, this card is about hope. The woman's nudity is a symbol not of sex but of trust in and unity with her surroundings. The image is a calming one, promising much for the future. Of course even hope can be misplaced and lead to ill-advised actions but this card is almost impossible to see badly.

Its astrological attribution is Aquarius, not the most obvious candidate since it is a sign originally ruled by Saturn. The modern rulership of Uranus, though, gives us a clue. Uranus is the planet of innovators and mavericks, those who depart from tested and trusted ways to try something new. These people depend on hope above all.

Exercise XVII: Recognising The Species
This exercise is very simple at one level and can get very complex at another. It is designed to help break down one of the biggest walls that stand between us and greatness.

The first part is to choose somebody famous that you admire. If possible this should be someone who is alive now or has been alive for a significant part of your lifetime. What they are famous for matters little as long as you sincerely admire it.

Once you have decided on a person, obtain and read his or her biography. I would suggest avoiding autobiographies for this purpose, although if one exists and you are interested enough you could read that as well and compare the two.

While reading, pay particular attention to the person's human failings. Look for failures before their eventual success. Look also for signs of irritability or other character defects. Notice where there were gambles and things that could have gone horribly wrong. In short, show yourself that this person was human, with the same three kilograms of brain and the same problems as the rest of us.

If it is possible to meet the person, so much the better. I have been lucky enough to meet a few of the famous people I admire, as well as one or two for whom I have little respect. Either way it is an empowering experience. To realise, for example, that my favourite musician has bad hair days and is rather shy makes me feel a lot closer to him. I may never write a song as brilliant as his but, on the other hand, I just might.

Lesson Eighteen

Elemental Dignities

This deceptively simple technique was first brought to my attention by Paul Hughes-Barlow, who is the leading authority on it. Paul's own book, *Tarot and the Magus* (Aeon Books 2003), covers the subject in greater detail than it is possible to do here. Since I have some grounding in Astrology, I found I had been using it to some extent unconsciously for years. Conscious awareness, however, makes it more useful.

As I said, the basic principle is very simple. The four elements tend to either strengthen each other or cancel each other out. Fire and Air are a strong combination, as are Earth and Water. All other combinations are weakened by conflict.

At this point the elemental attributions of the cards naturally become highly relevant. Those of the Minor Arcana are obvious by suit. Those Major Arcana that are assigned to a sign or explicitly to an element are also obvious but this leaves the seven planetary cards. For these I would suggest the following attributions:

| Fire | The Sun and The Tower |
| Water | The High Priestess and The Empress |

Air	The Magician
Earth	The World and The Wheel of Fortune

These are fairly tenuous and open to question and introduce a slight imbalance in the number of cards attributed to each element. However, they will serve in order to make a start.

It is easiest to see the dynamic of Elemental Dignities in a three-card spread. Suppose I am reading on a love issue for a lady and have drawn the King of Wands, flanked by the Two and Five of Cups. Looking at this at a non-ED level I would see the King as representing the partner, who is well centred in his own power and could come across as a little overbearing. The Two clearly points to a strong potential for a very positive relationship, while the Five seems to indicate that this ideal has not yet been reached.

Adding the ED level, my first observation is that we have a mixture of Fire and Water, which is guaranteed to be somewhat turbulent. (This has nothing to do with the partners' Sun signs, being purely a matter of the cards brought up.) Water predominates so we can expect the relationship to be emotion-led. Since the other element present is Fire, we can expect a strong sexual dynamic and perhaps some anger issues emerging.

Another aspect of Elemental Dignities is the importance of missing elements. In this case these are Air and Earth. Air is the element of intellect and logic and Earth is that of the material realm. Applying this to the situation, we can say that the problems in the relationship are aggravated by a lack of rational communication and practical thinking. An increase in these things, which may not be easy but is a definable and realistic goal, will help to give the relationship a more defined shape and balance out the problems. If I felt it was appropriate, I might go further and suggest some airy and/or earthy activities for the couple to share. These may be very symbolic or very literal. A course in philosophy or a skydiving session would both be good examples of experiencing the element of Air.

Using the same principle in a larger spread, it only takes a moment (with practice) to spot any major elemental trends. If you use the 15-card Romany layout it is also possible to look at the whole spread as a series of 3-card spreads and apply the system much as I have here. This could vastly increase the detail available from a comparatively simple spread.

The Planetary Relationship Spread

This is obviously an adaptation of the previous spread to focus specifically on relationships. As with other relationship spreads, sometimes the fact of one party being willing to spend time doing a reading often conveys information to the other party which helps to fix problems in itself.

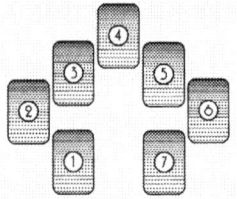

Moon - The emotional ebb and flow of the relationship
Mercury - Communication between the partners
Venus - Attractive and positive factors
Sun - Individual self-expression
Mars - Unattractive or negative factors
Jupiter - Future growth of the relationship
Saturn - Restrictions from outside factors

The Moon

Perhaps the easiest way to get a sense of this card's significance is to look at the literal Moon's place in our planetary view. We know that the Moon reflects the Sun's light, creating no light of its own, yet we talk about moonlight as if it were a separate thing, which in some ways it is. We know that the Moon is smaller than the Earth and far smaller than the Sun and yet, subjectively, it appears larger than the Sun. We also know that the Moon affects the tides of the sea and some of the most convincing evidence in favour of astrology comes from accident and crime statistics around a New or Full Moon.

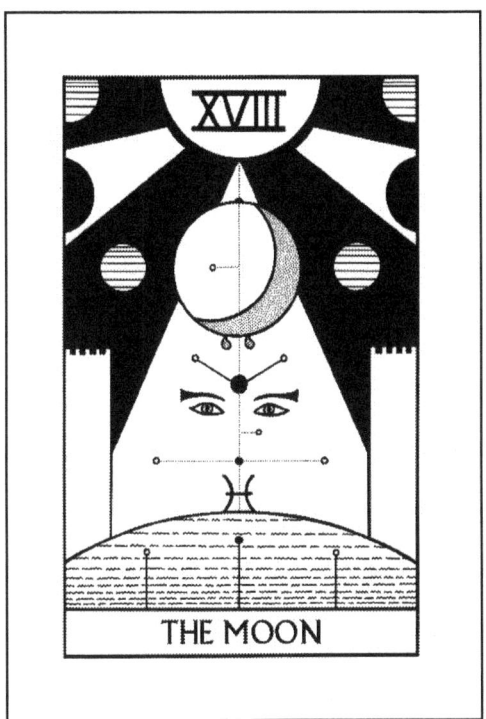

So how does this relate to Tarot? As I see it the first two parts show the Moon's capacity to cast illusions. When the Moon card appears I look for areas where the querent may be misinformed or come to wrong conclusions.

I also see this card as denoting strong emotions, good or bad. Can anyone be unaware of the emotional power of moonlight? The origins of the word 'lunatic', meaning one who is affected by the Moon, show that these matters are not necessarily benign and romantic, as well as uniting the two meanings discussed so far.

Another layer of meaning, linking back to the first, is creativity. A novel, play, movie or painting leads us (if it is good enough) into a voluntary illusion, a world of the artist's making. Even a photographic image, though based directly on a physical reality, is not identical to that reality.

Our final stop is in the world of dreams. These may not be as unreal as diehard materialists would have us believe, but they are certainly non-corporeal, creative, emotional and psychologically revealing. If you keep a dream journal and have not already tried this, you may find it rewarding to look at the tone of your dreams in relation to the lunar phases.

The astrological attribution is Pisces, one of the 'double signs' who can seem so contradictory to others. The sign is often linked to issues involving alcohol and drugs, which are distorting lenses, and to creativity.

Exercise XVIII: Acting Out

There are several different ways you could use this exercise, depending on your circumstances. Choose whichever seems most useful to you.

Think of a situation you are going to have to deal with in the near future which is uncomfortable for you. This could be a trivial level of irritation or major nerves. Now think of someone who would handle it easily and perhaps even enjoy it. This could be a friend, a famous person, a fictional character or even yourself at a different time. Then go and do whatever it is as that person.

A practical example may help. Recently I had to go to a shopping centre. This particular place is the kind that kids love but adults hate. So I decided to be a kid. Before and after doing what I had to do there I did things like buying myself an ice cream and looking at all the garish displays that kids love. I came out of that place grinning from ear to ear.

Another example would be a job interview or a driving test. Rather than sit there being nervous, become that confident person playing the part of you for a day. This kind of mental flip takes a bit of practice but it is immensely useful.

Lesson Nineteen

Different Divinatory Systems
   With all the different systems and schools of thought available on psychic work, there is apt to be a certain amount of confusion in the minds of the general public as to what we do and how. It is therefore a good idea to have a working knowledge of the distinctions between different forms of divination. What follows here is a brief glossary of the most widely used terms, their accepted meanings and some of the false ideas put on them by outsiders.

   Astrology There are three major schools of Astrology; Western, Vedic and Chinese. None of these simply divide people up into twelve categories and tell all the people in each category the same stuff. While many Astrologers will have a working knowledge of Tarot and vice versa, this is by no means universal or necessary. Having said that, the dynamics of a reading with either are often very similar.

   Clairvoyant This term can be used as a catchall term for any of the arts in this list. 'Straight' clairvoyance, without any form of guides or physical tools, is perfectly possible for anyone with the guts to give it a try. Having said that, it can be hard work and in a formal reading context has a habit of straying into useless sidelines. It is superficially more impressive to the client and can have a lot of value but not more than a good reading using Tarot or other tools.

I Ching Seldom used in the West for commercial readings, this method is part of the Taoist culture, which embraces many different arts. It is best suited to specific questions rather than general readings. I love it, but it needs to be seen in the context of the broader Taoist philosophy.

Medium Basically, a medium is one who speaks to the departed, or sometimes to Spirit Guides. I started out with a lot of scepticism towards this form of work. I have since learned to respect it but it is different from other forms of psychic work and needs to be seen as such.

Psychic This word can refer to many different disciplines. Many non-specialists see it as synonymous with clairvoyance, which is more or less true, or with mediumship, which is a specialised form. To add to the confusion, the word is used quite differently in psychology and related disciplines to refer generally to the mental functions.

Runes These are best seen as a separate discipline altogether. I have great respect for this system but every attempt I have seen to put Tarot and Runes together seems to degrade both. Having said that, the Runes are perhaps the closest to Tarot of all the systems here in terms of the dynamic process of a reading and the two-edged nature of the tool itself. The misuse by the Nazis of various Runic symbols has led to some very unfair prejudice against the Nordic system in general, which is now thankfully dying out and allowing the system to come to prominence again.

The Planetary Business Spread

I feel a curious mixture of emotions when somebody comes to me for a reading on a new business venture. On the one hand, I am philosophically in favour of everybody being self-employed and, having been so myself for a number of years, I would not readily return to employee status. On the other hand, I know the pain that can come to those who have the courage to take charge of their own destiny at this level. This spread was designed to try to address the issues facing anyone taking this risky decision. I have found it effective in helping them to avoid some of the pitfalls and to build on solid ground.

The cards are read as follows:-
1. The core business idea.
2. Advertising and marketing.
3. Cashflow.
4. Factors in favour.
5. Factors against.
6. Growth potential.
7. Legal considerations.

The Sun

Once again we can turn to astronomy for our chief clue to the nature of this card. The Sun is nearer to us by far than any of the stars we see in the night sky and far more important in our day-to-day lives. Apart from the chemical energy inherent in the matter on our planet, the Sun is our only significant energy source. Without it our planet would be nothing more than a big lump of rock, cold and inert.

The Sun in the Tarot sense is about positivity and joy. I see it as giving here and now what is promised for future delivery by the Star. This card is about as positive as it gets in the Tarot universe. Another link with the Star is that this card often

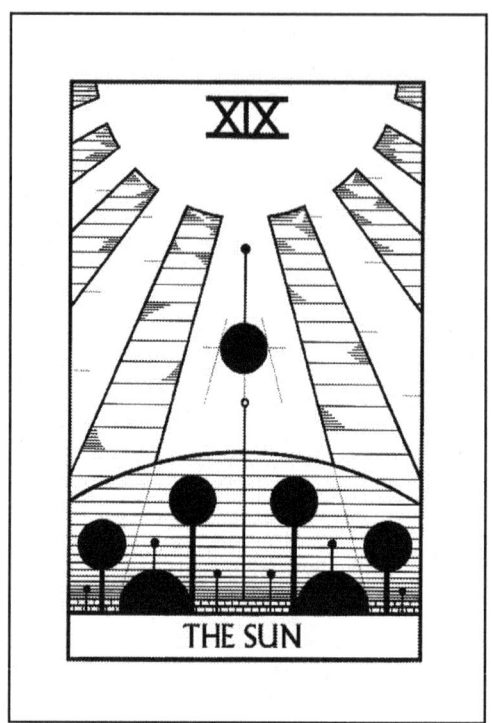

shows people ~ sometimes a couple, sometimes a child on a horse or a little boy and girl ~ and they are usually naked. Once again, the reason for the nudity is not sex but trust and comfort.

The astrological attribution here is the obvious one, the Sun. An astrologer sees the Sun as the 'central self' into whom we grow as we live our lives.

Exercise XIX: Reasons To Be Cheerful

This exercise is short and simple, although it is worth taking your time about it. Simply sit down with your preferred beverage and a notebook and jot down all the things you like about your life right now. Keep the phrasing positive and make it fun. Notice how you feel immediately after doing this. Notice also how people react to you while you are in that state of mind.

Lesson Twenty

Recommended Reading

While this book should be all you need to get started reading the cards there are one or two gems out there which can considerably extend your knowledge. One book that should be read by anyone who is serious about Tarot is *The Book of Thoth* by Aleister Crowley. This masterwork is still as relevant today as it was when it was written.

All of Gareth Knight's works are worth reading. The two most relevant to Tarot readers are *The Magical World of the Tarot* and *The Treasure House of Images*.

The Truth About The Tarot by Gerald Suster is a favourite of mine. Based strongly on Crowley's work, it offers some valuable insights.

The Inner Guide Meditation by Edwin C. Steinbrecher is not strictly a Tarot book but explains a great deal about archetypes and a valid method of working with them.

My colleague Paul Hughes-Barlow's book *Tarot and the Magus* is excellent. His original approach, combined with a great respect for Crowley and the Golden Dawn have produced a book well worth studying.

On Other Subjects

I regard Aleister Crowley with great respect, not least as a literary stylist. His many books are all worth reading. None are easy reading but that is in line with the complexity and immense value of his chosen subjects.

Robert Anton Wilson is another thought-provoking writer. A master of non-fiction and experimental fiction.

Tony Buzan writes exceedingly well on mnemonics and other thinking tools. My own discussion of mnemonics in these pages owes much to his writings.

The Compass Rose Spread

This is a spread I devised primarily for reading for myself, though I see no reason why it should not be used for others. It is designed for those situations which, no matter what your philosophical or spiritual perspective, are basically a royal pain. The idea is to get the life lesson and find your way out of the situation as quickly as possible.

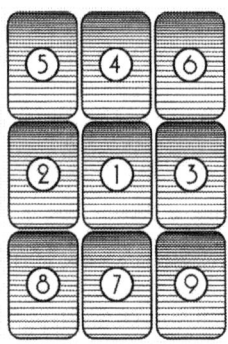

Card 1 represents the problem. You can either choose a significator (any card in the deck but most likely a pip card) to represent the problem or leave it to chance, which can be illuminating.

Cards 4, 3, 7 and 2 represent North, East, South and West respectively, and their corresponding elements; in order, these are Earth, Air, Water and Fire. If your problem includes an element of location, these cards may provide a simple solution very quickly. If not, I trust that by now you are familiar enough with the four elements to make an interpretation of them.

Card 5 represents a respected elder, perhaps a parent or teacher, and how they might tackle the situation. We are not aspiring to mediumship here, or to realistic representation of the person. As such, if necessary, a fictional character can be used.

Card 6 balances this with a figure held in contempt. Again, if you have spent your life surrounded by living saints, a fictional character may be used. Sometimes the insight of looking at things through the eyes of someone we normally see as evil or stupid can bring exactly the insight we lack.

Card 9 answers the question 'How could I make things worse?' Once again, we are applying an indirect approach, hoping that this will give us the insight we need to make things better.

With Card 8, we give Dame Fortune a place to speak. We do not need to believe literally in blind fate here; the fact that some forces are beyond our knowing makes them close enough to randomness for our purposes.

Finally, if all else fails, return to Card 1 and meditate upon it for a while. It is surprising how often this will provide a solution.

Judgement

At first glance this card seems to show a traditional Christian image of a kind that even some modern Christians might reject. The Archangel Gabriel sounds the trumpet and a man, woman and child rise naked from their graves. Here the nudity takes on another shade of meaning, reflecting the idea that we shall enter the next world as we entered this one, naked and without possessions. Some more modern interpretations retitle the card 'Karma'.

To me this card is about laws; not the personal self-limitation of The Devil or the social laws of Justice but the laws of the physical realm, those being discovered by science and those acknowledged by metaphysicians as 'God's laws'.

In practice Judgement often shows up when the querent can do little or nothing to change the situation and must wait for a change in 'outer' circumstances. However much we may believe intellectually that we all create, and can therefore change, our reality, we all hit blocks. Sometimes this turns out well, producing benefits we could not have consciously dreamed up for ourselves. At other times it adds to our burden.

Crowley renames this card The Aeon. Aeonics are a key concept in his work and, as you might expect, his version of the card shows several of his favourite symbols. Thoth is shown, along with the winged disc of Ra and the goddess Nuit forming an arch over the main body of the card.

The astrological attribution here is the element of Fire. Symbolically and practically, fire is a cleansing agent. It is also the finest of the four elements, showing that the highest and strongest forces are at work.

Exercise XX: Personal Aeonics

Imagine that you are making notes for an autobiography. Identify the different periods in your life, the things which started and ended them, the themes of places and people as contributors to your life (whether positive or negative) and the difference they made.

Observe also your own attitude, then and now, to these different periods, situations and people. It may also be worth looking at what your attitude might have been had you done this exercise somewhere between the original incidents and now. While 'test driving' this exercise, I was pleasantly surprised to find that certain episodes which used to evoke anger in me now produce no reaction.

One of your most important tools in gaining value from this exercise is compassion, both for others and for yourself. Be aware that there were reasons for the actions of all concerned. I certainly look at my past with bafflement at my capacity for missing opportunities. However, the fact that I feel this is in itself an indication of my progress and the psychological weight I have lifted from my shoulders.

Having said that, this exercise is not necessarily particularly flattering or ego boosting and can be quite emotionally intense. If you are currently suffering from low self-esteem or a delicate emotional balance, this is one to delay until you feel stronger.

Lesson Twenty One

Reading Professionally
At this stage you may be thinking about the possibilities of a career in Tarot. Let me tell you the bad news first. There is not much money in it. A certain amount depends on where you are and how you go about it but I have yet to meet a seriously rich Tarot reader. I have met quite a few who had money problems and have had my share of 'day jobs' in the past myself. The other bad news is that if this course has been your introduction to Tarot it will be a few years of practice before you are ready to offer a professional service.

On the other hand, reading Tarot is such a satisfying job that I for one cannot imagine going back to a 'proper' job. The main types of reading, in terms of the professional mechanics, are:

Home visits Whether you are visiting your clients' homes or they yours, you need to be mindful of both your personal safety and your clients' emotional comfort. Horror stories, accurate or otherwise, are rare but they do happen and even false ones do our reputation no good at all.

Speaking personally, I hardly ever invite clients to my home. This is partly for privacy and partly to avoid clients making an appointment and then failing to turn up. I have often visited clients in their homes and have always had positive experiences when doing so.

Public places (including psychic fairs) This can work surprisingly well. The obvious concern is privacy but I find most people will respect the process even if they are not Tarot fans. In the case of a psychic fair you have the added advantage of meeting colleagues from whom you may learn something about either reading or presentation.

At the risk of stating the obvious, if you arrange to read for a client in a pub, cafe, restaurant or similar, do check the attitude of the management first. Objections may not be purely a matter of prejudice. Commercial premises can have some odd restrictions placed by landlords or local authorities.

Premium-rate telephone lines This way of working can test your ego strength to the maximum. Clients can be drunk or just plain stupid and feel free to abuse the faceless voice at the other end of the line. There are also the ones who will simply put the receiver down as soon as they hear your voice.

There are also unscrupulous lines out there. One of these nearly landed me in the street or the bankruptcy court when their financial mismanagement came back to haunt them. Some have no apparent ethics at all and define 'quality' in a reader entirely by average call duration.

Having said that, I am currently doing a lot of work for a line whose ethics are impeccable and whose pay rate is among the best in the UK. They leave me alone to do what I do best and pay me punctually for doing it. The quantity of work is as consistent as humanly possible and the management were very understanding when sudden health problems prevented me from fulfilling my commitments for a few days.

The big plus with this kind of work is in working from home. I can be at work ten seconds after getting out of bed and nobody cares how I look as long as I do my job right. Also, between calls, I can play with my pets, practice my music or even cook. Much of this book was written between calls.

Post or email   This is my least favourite method. There is nothing wrong with it in a technical sense and I suppose it helps to counteract bias. However, the interaction is very impersonal. There is also the problem of how much to write. How many words equal a life situation? Also, although I love writing, it takes much more time than talking. This can kill some of the spontaneity on which a good reading depends. If you want to work by post, my advice is to invest in a professional-quality tape recorder.

Pricing   If you are working for a telephone service they dictate your rates. Otherwise, my advice is to match your competitors. Besides keeping things friendly, this gives an impression of confidence. Pricing too low will not increase your trade. Remember, no matter what you charge, some will think it too high, some too low.

Refunds   Even if you feel you have given a good reading, if the client does not, I suggest you refund or decline to take their money. This shows integrity and can even produce extra business.

The Pyramid Spread

This deceptively simple spread works on the idea of the four elements and the corresponding idea of the Four Worlds used in Kabalah. These can be thought of as levels through which anything passes on its way to manifestation in the physical universe, in much the same way as we looked at the Sephiroth on our journey through the pip cards.

What makes it dynamically different from the Tree of Life spread is the apparent change of emphasis and the grouping of cards. I say 'apparent' because the top level of one card is not less important than the bottom layer of four. One of my favourite spiritual ideas (first heard from Harry Palmer, creator of the excellent Avatar course) is that if things are getting simpler you are on the right track. Thus there is little need to go on at length about the highest levels, but more room for complication lower down.

I like this spread primarily for examining specific projects, either at the planning stage or, more commonly, halfway through when some of the obstacles have become apparent.

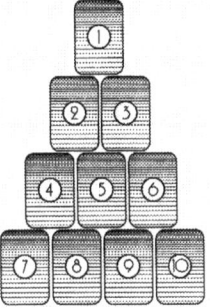

The first card represents Atziluth, the world of pure spirit, and the element of Fire. For our purposes it can be seen as the basic idea behind the project. The card here may represent that idea pure and simple or may highlight something particularly right or wrong about it.

Cards 2 and 3 represent Briah, the creative world, and the element of Water. The two cards here can be thought of as representing the binary force of creation ñ Sun/Moon, Yin/Yang, God/Goddess, or however you see it according to your structure of beliefs. These may be working well together or may be at odds, which we can ascertain using Elemental Dignities.

Cards 4, 5 and 6 represent Yetzirah, the formative or mental world, and the element of Air. There are innumerable trinities in the various pantheons that would fit here. My favourite, taken from psychoanalysis, is that of Id, Ego and Superego.

Cards 7, 8, 9 and 10 represent Assiah, the material world, and the element of Earth. Here again we have the happy 'coincidence' that there are four cards, which could represent a further subdivision into the four elements.

Of course each layer also works as a group and even looking at the interplay of colours in the whole spread as a kind of mandala can be effective in producing insight.

Incidentally, it is worth mentioning that the number of cards in the bottom layer of a triangle of this kind will always equal the number of layers. Thus, it would be possible to devise a pyramid spread of five layers based on Chinese or Discordian ideas, or indeed any number that takes your fancy up to 12. This last would use all 78 cards.

The World

At the end of the cycle of the Major Arcana, fittingly enough, we have a symbol of completion. In traditional decks, a central figure dances inside a wreath, around which the Kerubim look on. Although it usually looks female, the dancing figure is described in several sources as a hermaphrodite. This makes symbolic sense, adding to the sense of completion.

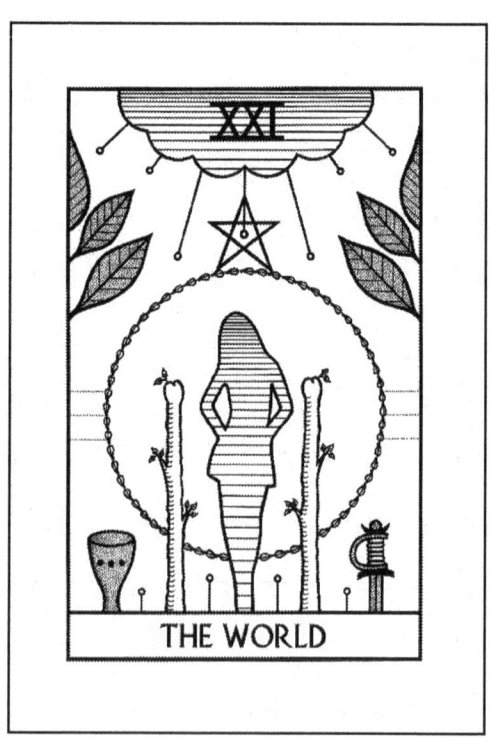

At the most mundane level this card can literally refer to travel. Looking more esoterically, it shows completion of a project or the successful outcome of an episode in life. Sometimes we can have it all and this card shows us those times.

The astrological attribution of Saturn may seem to contradict this. Yet if we see Saturn as the Lord of Limits it makes sense. Can we honestly say we know it all before we reach our limits?

Exercise XXI: Sharing Consciousness

Here I have saved the best until last. This exercise, followed repeatedly in different circumstances, is a key to a great many things. I first came across it in a novel, *Stranger in a Strange Land* by Robert Heinlein (which is, incidentally, a superb read). There it is known as Grokking. Serge Kahili King uses the same name for it in his book *Urban Shaman*. It is also referred to obliquely in various occult texts and appears in a modified (but perfectly workable) form in Terry Pratchett's Discworld novels as Borrowing.

Pick an object. I would suggest something inanimate and fairly simple in form at first, perhaps a crystal or an ornament. Hold it and try to simply observe its physical form for a few moments. Then mentally 'enter' the object. At first this will be an effort of imagination. As soon as you attain a reasonable degree of success move on to another object. Eventually you will find yourself spontaneously 'entering' the object with little effort and perhaps with a few surprises. Notice, for example, the difference between manmade and natural substances.

When you feel confident of your ability to do this consistently with inanimate objects, try plants, animals and then human beings. Again, expect surprises. The Universe is full of consciousness, indeed is nothing but consciousness, and we can make direct contact with any part of it if we choose to do so.

Afterword

Earlier I spoke of the Tarot deck as a map of human life. Another analogy that works equally well is that of a menu. The way most people live their lives is like going into a restaurant, refusing to look at the menu and shouting 'Just give me food!' We can hardly blame the Universal Waiter if, under these circumstances, he brings us something not to our taste or beyond our budget.

As I hope I have illustrated here, Tarot can be very effective both as a menu for our life choices and, to push the analogy a little further, as a restaurant guide so that we choose the right place for the kind of food we want. If what you really fancy is a good curry, you are serving neither yourself nor Universal Wellbeing by walking into an Italian place. At the ultimate level we dictate our own menu, as well as the decor, music, seating plan and waiting staff.

If you have gained as much knowledge and happiness by reading and working with this course as I have by writing it then I have achieved what I set out to do. I wish you joy in your life and in your relationship with Tarot. This I wish in a spirit of enlightened self-interest, knowing that the more happy people there are in this world the easier it will be for each one of us to be happy.

Appendix One

Aleister Crowley and the Law of Thelema

Even in the nebulous world of occultism, which has long delighted the gutter press with its secrecy and consequent capacity for salacious mythmaking on their part, nobody has had as much nonsense talked and written about him as Aleister Crowley. It is certainly true that he deliberately encouraged this for reasons of his own but those of us who have derived some of our ideas from his owe it to him and to future fellow-travellers to try to present the truth.

As others have observed, Crowley's 'excesses' amounted to nothing more than would be expected of any rock star. He was bisexual, which was considerably more of a big deal then than now, and he experimented with drugs long enough ago that there were some legitimate questions to be answered by their use.

What really annoyed people about Crowley was his common sense. Thelema, the philosophy of Magick and of life which he presented, is simply too practical for those who like their spirituality divorced from the physical world. The few times anything along those lines has been attempted in a group setting, it has worked very well.

According to Crowley, the Book of the Law, which is at the core of his work, was not his invention but was dictated to him by a spirit called Aiwass, who was brought to his attention by his first wife Rose while they were on their honeymoon in Egypt. He was initially disinclined to take the dictation and fought somewhat against the content, since he was at that time a Buddhist. However, his Golden Dawn training enabled him to test this spirit somewhat and the spirit passed these tests with flying colours. It was still some years before Crowley started working seriously on developing the concepts outlined in the book.

The most often quoted statement in the Book of the Law is 'Do what thou wilt shall be the whole of the law.' At first sight this looks like simple hedonism but there is more to it than that. Thelema asserts that we all have a True Will, as distinctly individual as our faces but nonetheless in harmony with everyone else's True Will. We are all born aware of this True Will, at least at an instinctive level, but our awareness of it becomes cluttered and confused by our conditioning. Thus, the Great Work becomes a process of removing or seeing beyond this conditioning to the person we were designed to be and living accordingly.

Readers who are familiar with psychoanalysis or other healing disciplines may sense here a similarity with the theory that seems to be basic to all such disciplines. This idea of a blueprint of perfection muddied and distorted by a wicked world also seems to be a part of conventional religion. What is unique about Crowley's philosophy is its focus on individual freedom. Freud, for example, may have proposed a (then) rather scandalous focus on sex in his theories but his practical work was geared towards fitting the individual into society. Crowley says that if the individual is genuinely working in line with his True Will and finds himself at odds with society then it is society that is out of line.

Another frequently quoted line from the Book of the Law is 'Every man and woman is a star.' In other words, just as the gravitational pull of each star and planet in the galaxy plays its part in holding the whole together, so each man and woman has an essential role to play in society. Hopefully this is a statement of the obvious to most modern readers but in a time thirty years before Hitler came to power the idea that a particular ethnic or social group was responsible for most or all of the problems in the world and could be eliminated to advantage was more credible to many people. The statement also asserts a fundamentally equal level of importance for everyone in the natural scheme of things, negating the 'master and slave' mentality implicit in the imperialist worldview and still alive today even in socialist philosophies, which replace the individual master with a collective one.

At this point you may or may not agree with the ideas stated. I hope you would at least agree that this style of living has not been tried on the mass scale. Our present society is built around the idea that people need protecting from themselves. This seems to remain true whatever the prevailing political style. As The Who said years ago, 'Meet the new boss, same as the old boss.'

So what can we do to change this? I believe, and many spiritual teachers have stated, that in order to change the world we must first change ourselves. I hope I have shown you how Tarot can be a powerful tool for self-liberation and for helping others to liberate themselves. This is no small thing in itself as people who are free and happy tend to be role models for others, as well as being uninterested in controlling others' behaviour. Freedom and happiness are, I believe, ultimately more effective cultural viruses than slavery and misery.

Joining an occult order or other spiritual organisation may be effective for some. I hold no brief for any particular one of these, since I am not a member of any myself at this time. In any case, I do not feel that this is the place to proselytise for such bodies.

Looking at the semi-collective level, there are certainly places where attempts have been made to honour individual freedom in a collective environment. Two of these come to mind, both initiated from a secular perspective and for secular goals. That fact makes them all the more worthy of observation from a spiritual perspective.

A. S. Neill founded Summerhill School in 1921. His idea was to remove compulsion entirely from the life and education of children, giving them the freedom and dignity to grow naturally according to their own instincts. At his school, which still exists, lessons are not compulsory and collective decisions are made by a meeting (originally weekly, but at the time of writing held four times a week), at which all present have an equal vote, from the youngest pupil to the head. All rules are subject to change at these meetings.

Conventional 'wisdom' would expect life at such a school to be chaotic and disruptive to the development of young people. The opposite appears to be the case. Order and common sense prevail and bullying, the constant companion of my own schooldays at a 'good' grammar school, seems to be almost unheard of. In short, giving power and responsibility to young children is not a recipe for a 'Lord of the Flies' disaster but for their growth into mature, responsible adults via a happy, safe and rewarding childhood, just as the Law of Thelema would predict.

Our second example comes from a world which Crowley as an individual despised, that of commerce. On this point I differ from Crowley and enjoy observing and participating in the money game, especially when those I see as the 'good guys' win. Ricardo Semler and his company, Semco, strike me as an excellent example of what can happen when the profit motive and personal values work together rather than in competition.

Founded in the 1950s, Semco started out as a small engineering firm and grew through the 1960s with the growth of the Brazilian shipbuilding industry. That growth proved short-lived and when Ricardo Semler took the firm over from his father in 1980 it was in trouble. Semler took immediate and drastic action, firing many of the management team and diversifying the company's activities. He kept the company running on a wing and a prayer for long enough to see these changes take effect and then began to make more unconventional changes.

The focus of these changes was on devolving power and responsibility from the CEO and Board of Directors down to the individual employees. They varied from seemingly cosmetic changes such as getting rid of strict dress codes to allowing workers to set their own pay rates. Later initiatives included helping employees to become self-employed subcontractors. These changes have helped Semco to survive in the Brazilian economy, one of the most volatile in the world.

Some of the opposition to these changes tells us almost as much about human nature as their success. For example, when Semler decided to dispose of the security guards searching each employee at the end of the working day, the workers and unions opposed him. They felt that the inevitably greater levels of staff pilferage would lead to false accusations and bad feeling between people. They wanted to be searched so they could prove their innocence.

To this day, Semco continues to evolve towards greater levels of democracy and employee involvement. It also continues to survive and thrive in an environment where many companies have gone to the wall through sheer economic turbulence. We do not need much knowledge of economics to see a relationship between these facts.

What these examples show is that individual empowerment tends not to disrupt social harmony but to augment it. It seems that people cooperate and contribute to society not because of rigid social structures but in spite of them.

It might appear to some that I am simply reinventing the principles of anarchy here. This is not so. I believe that societies of all types need structure, but that if we wish to see a society thrive we must remember that it consists of individuals and give them the space they need to grow. I believe that the political and economic structures of today will look as outdated and pointlessly restrictive to our descendants as the hierarchies of Feudal England or Confucian China do to us today. These changes will not happen through the barrel of a gun but through individual self-evolution and simply getting out of each other's way.

This brings us to the third core statement from the Book of the Law: 'Love is the law, love under will.' The word 'love' here has little connection to the word as used in everyday life. It refers to all interaction, whether 'loving' in a conventional sense or not. As I see it, this injunction states that it is necessary to make our outer world interaction consistent with our True Will. This interaction will then naturally be consistent not only with our own highest good but with that of all concerned.

Much more could be said about Thelema but I have said enough to show its relationship to the main subject of this book. I hope I have also said enough for the reader to pursue the subject further. It is fascinating and rewarding at many levels.

Appendix Two

Constructing the Inner Temple

The original plan for this appendix was to write a pathworking (a kind of imaginative journey) covering all of the Major Arcana and building up an inner landscape. You could return to this landscape at any time in the future in order to work on problems or projects in company with the archetypes of the Major Arcana as they exist within you. This style of approach has been used many times before, from the earliest mystery religions through great thinkers of the Renaissance such as John Dee and Giordano Bruno to modern authors such as Dolores Ashcroft-Nowicki and Gareth Knight. It certainly works well and would have been fun to write and, hopefully, to read.

However, when I came to sit down and write it, it occurred to me that anybody capable of making use of such an inner space should be equally capable of constructing it for themselves. By doing so they would gain the advantages of a structure custom-built to their own specification, taking account of their own likes and dislikes and, perhaps more importantly, their own layers of personal significance for each item placed there. For example, to one person, a castle may bring forth images of spectacular adventure and a positive feeling of excitement.

To another, the same castle may conjure a feeling of violent death in the terrifying close-quarters battles for which castles were devised.

So what do you need to construct your inner temple? Looking at physical tools first, I would suggest a pen and paper and a Tarot deck as the minimum requirement. If you enjoy making pictures or models, some suitable tools for those activities may also be valuable. For the initial construction, the correspondences given in this book should be adequate to devise the most vital components linking this inner place to the esoteric structure of the Tarot. If you wish to make it more complete at a later date, the Tables of Correspondence found in *Liber 777* by Aleister Crowley or the various tables scattered throughout the various books on the Order of the Golden Dawn would be useful. However, at first I would suggest keeping the whole thing as simple as possible.

The first thing you need is a structure. This needs to have at least twenty-two distinct spaces within it, and possibly thirty-two to accommodate the whole of the Major and Minor Arcana, so a flat or small house is not likely to be adequate. If it can take the shape of the Tree of Life, this is an added advantage. A large country house and grounds might work well, as would a castle. A small village could be used, with twenty-two paths or roads and ten houses. You could set the whole thing outdoors, perhaps in a forest, or go to the opposite extreme with an elaborate system of underground rooms and tunnels. A space station would be perfectly workable. It is all down to personal preference.

Once you have a broad idea of the style and structure of your temple, you can build it up gradually over time. Starting with the entrance at Malkuth, you could build that area in a way that reflects the sense of groundedness of that Sephira and the relevant cards, in this case the Tens and Pages/Princesses. The room itself could be square, with one wall in each of the four colours of that sphere in the Queen Scale (citrine, olive, russet and black). Pictures and other decorations could supply further imagery. Even a relevant incense could be used to enhance the atmosphere of the room.

Continuing our progress, the next step would be the Path of The World, which of course may be a path or a corridor according to earlier choices. The relevant colour would be black, perhaps supplied by a deep night sky or walls painted with images of constellations. There should also, of course, be some representation of The World card somewhere on this path, preferably about halfway along it. This leads to Yesod, for which the colour is violet and a circular shape would fit well for the lunar attribution of the Sephira. Yesod is sometimes known as the Treasure House of Images, so we might choose to deck this room out as an art gallery. This would make it easy to show pictures relevant to the four Nines.

We can continue in this fashion throughout the Tree, perhaps making Hod a library, Netzach a comfortable lounge or ornamental garden, and so on. These can be used in different ways according to their nature and the needs of the moment. Suppose, for example, you have a new work colleague with whom you are not getting on. You could go to the lounge or garden at Netzach and have a discussion with that person in that safe space. This may sound rather childish and one-sided but I have used techniques of this kind to deal with problems with colleagues, relatives, partners and even, on one occasion, a pet dog. The dog showed the most dramatic positive change of the lot, perhaps because the conscious and subconscious are better connected in children and animals than in 'sophisticated' human adults.

Sometimes the most valuable aspect of this astral temple is the way that it can develop a seemingly independent life of its own and change in ways that are not planned or foreseen by the creator. Authors of fiction often describe something similar happening, with characters taking over and forming the plot into something not originally planned by the author. In this case we are almost inviting this to happen by connecting with the archetypes on the Astral Plane, which is their home territory. If one of them is behaving in a way you find unacceptable, it is wise to negotiate rather than try to impose your will.

Once you have built this personal space, it is wise to visit it every day, even if you do not have anything specific to do there. Visualisation as a skill has much in common with music and even the best players become rusty if denied the opportunity to practice.

www.ingramcontent.com/pod-product-compliance
Ingram Content Group UK Ltd.
Pitfield, Milton Keynes, MK11 3LW, UK
UKHW041914140426
5217IPUK00013B/151